Spa: The Sensuous Experience
Robert D. Henry and Julie D. Taylor

Visit some of these delicious sites & partake in their wonderful treatments!

Healthy Regards,

Robert Henry

Published in Australia in 2005 by
The Images Publishing Group Pty Ltd
ABN 89 059 734 431
6 Bastow Place, Mulgrave, Victoria 3170, Australia
Tel: +61 3 9561 5544 Fax: +61 3 9561 4860
books@images.com.au
www.imagespublishing.com

Copyright © The Images Publishing Group Pty Ltd 2005
The Images Publishing Group Reference Number: 575

National Library of Australia
Cataloguing-in-Publication entry:
Henry, Robert D.
Spa: the sensuous experience.
ISBN 1 920744 40 1.
1. Architecture and recreation.
2. Recreational therapy.
I. Taylor, Julie D. II. Title.

725.73

Coordinating Editor: Robyn Beaver
Designed by John and Orna Designs, London
Film by Mission Productions Limited, Hong Kong
Printed by Everbest Printing Co Ltd, Hong Kong/China

IMAGES has included on its website a page for special notices in relation
to this and our other publications. Please visit www.imagespublishing.com.

We dedicate this book to the caregivers who slather, stroke, and soothe
our imperfect bodies into perfect states of bliss.

The Spa at Four Seasons Resort Chiang Mai. Photo: Luca Tettoni

Spa: The Sensuous Experience

Robert D. Henry and Julie D. Taylor

Contents

Spa descriptions by Julie D. Taylor

Spa State of Mind by Robert D. Henry

The sensuous "Hall of Whispers" at Ajune. Photo: Dan Bibb

What accounts for the explosive re-emergence of the 2,000-year-old spa experience? The baby boom contingent is entering mid-life adolescence, where the possibility of becoming a centenarian is a national obsession. Couple this with a desire for a vigorous quality of life, and we begin to understand the demand for longevity-enhancing regimens. People not only want to live longer, but they expect to be able to enjoy a sumptuous meal, indulge their greatest passions, and maintain an active lifestyle well into their 90s. The new paradigm is "inner well-being radiates outer beauty." Thus, the adage "if you look good, you feel good" has been superseded.

Today, we visit a spa for different reasons from those of preceding generations. The European cure or weight-loss programs have been supplanted by destination spa packages, wellness spa experiences, exotic resort and hotel spas, time-sensitive day spas, classic thalasso and thermal spas, and yes, even medical spas. These categories were non-existent a mere 15 years ago during the formation of the International Spa Association (ISPA). Further hybrids continue to surface today. Spas are providing the proactive remedy to our current cultural needs. They are here to stay and are fast becoming an integral part of our cultural condition.

Only 20 years ago, the idea of managing stress was probably not a part of your mindset—whether you were considered the sandbox set, the swinging set, or the shuffleboard set. Stress was a major killer of my father's generation. Unfortunately, in his day, smoking and drinking were how many people learned to spell relief. Even if I could have my dear father back, I'm not sure he'd be open to my weekly regimen: shiatsu massage, morning laps in the pool, weekend runs pushing a baby-jogger, or cuddling up with our selection of self-help and spiritually enlightening books.

Stress reduction is a premium benefit attributed to the spa experience. The exponential amount of change that we negotiate in our daily lives produces extraordinary levels of stress. Research has proven that the by-product of adapting to change results in stress for even the simplest of organisms. The toll it takes on our general health and well-being is considerable. Tremendous growth within all areas of the spa industry has been generated by proactive health measures that are successful in reducing stress. Offering an opportunity to unwind and relax—if only for an hour squeezed into our hectic schedules—spas provide solutions to our time pauperism.

The element of touch is primal and powerful, which is why spas are so important today. The digital workplace—complete with its revolutionary technology—distances us from interpersonal contact. Ironically, the more connected we are technologically, the more out of touch we are with our senses. It is our humanity that separates us from machines. Premature babies who are gently massaged in the nursery will develop more quickly than those left untouched or hooked up to machines. Human contact is essential to our health. Whenever my two-year-old daughter takes a tumble and gets a booboo, the first thing she shouts is "rub it!" A simple comforting touch reassures and restores her sense of well-being. I have found that whenever and wherever appropriate, instead of a handshake, I give a bear hug to friends and close acquaintances. This simple gesture has brought so much warmth and compassion to my relationships, both personal and professional. (Try it: you'll both feel better!)

Why is it—in our need to control our modern lives—that we have forsaken the very things that enrich and express our biological essence? The spa experience encourages us to celebrate our senses and get back in touch with the sensuous. In my architectural practice, the empirical experience (all that one can potentially see, hear, touch, taste, and smell) drives the design of our spas and has become the overriding aspect that links all of our creative work. What continues to delight us is the evolving nature of spas and their substantial contribution to the sensuous experience.

The History of Spa by Julie V. Iovine

Sybaritic or spiritual, for healing or for pure indulgence, taking the waters is a tradition transcending time, culture, and most inhibitions. There seem to be as many springs—some rich in sulphur and redolent of rotten eggs, others the color of emeralds or as effervescent as champagne—as there are fissures in the mountainous foothills gaping open to let them burst forth. And where geology hasn't made natural outlets, plumbing has found ways to supply even more bathing experiences that may have originated in a desire for cleanliness, but ultimately laid claims to a higher plateau of body-mind harmony.

There is really no recorded beginning to the history of taking the waters. Most likely, people learned from observing animals as they retreated to hot-spring-fed pools to cure themselves when they were wounded or ill. At many of Japan's thermal springs, it is still possible to watch monkeys soak. Paleolithic hunters bathed in the springs that became the legendary watering hole of Bath, England. The Egyptians, without access to the kind of terrain that produces natural springs, still took great pleasure in—and spent huge fortunes on—steeping themselves in baths of ass' milk, crushed strawberries, and spices. For the ancient Greeks, wrestling, philosophy, and bathing were pursuits that went hand-in-hand with the daily life of the truly sophisticated citizen.

Bath, England, home to Thermae Bath Spa. Photo: Matt Cardy

Julie V. Iovine is a senior reporter at *The New York Times*, and is the author of *Michael Graves: Compact Design Portfolio* (Chronicle Books), *Guggenheim Bilbao, Guggenheim New York* (Princeton Architectural Press), and *Chic Simple: Home* (Thames & Hudson). Her interest in spas as a cultural phenomenon was spurred by a chance visit to an abandoned spa in Curia, Portugal, in the 1980s. Since then she has traveled extensively to historic spas throughout Europe.

But, in the Western world, it was the Romans who turned taking the waters into both an art form and an essential luxury. The baths created to serve Roman soldiers as they made their way through Europe, Africa, and Asia Minor not only spread the tradition, but also established a network of bathing structures that remained intact for centuries, and are to this day rich mines of archeological information about the past.

Some say the word *spa*, which by now has become shorthand for an extraordinary range of bathing experiences, is an acronym for an expression from Nero's time, *salus per aqua* (health through water). However, the term might also have been appropriated from the watering hole and town of the same name in Belgium—Spa—which had its heyday in the early 17th century. However, no other society was as fixated by the ritual of public bathing as were the Romans.

During the reign of Augustus, around 12 BC, not long after Marcus Agrippa built the first true bathing complexes, called thermae, there were 381 miles (613 kilometers) of aqueducts bringing water to Rome to feed the city's 926 public baths and 11 imperial thermae. The consumption of water per person per day was 300 gallons, comparable to the amount used by a family of four today. The Diocletian Baths covered 32.5 acres (13 hectares) and could hold 6,000 people.

A stupendous ruin immortalized by Piranesi's etchings, the Diocletian Baths were more than palatial in their day. The walls were made of Egyptian marble. The floors were tiled and supplied with radiant heat, thanks to hot water channeled through sub-floor piping. For further enjoyment after a bath, there were libraries, galleries, a gym, and a stadium.

The daily ritual at the thermae was a social event, not only for the wealthiest, but for all citizens. Eventually, however, popularity attracted corruption. In an attempt to control and subdue the revelry for which the thermae became notorious, the mixing of the sexes, which had always been accepted, was outlawed. Late in the Empire, the baths themselves were condemned. The tradition of bathing fell into neglect.

It was not until after the crusades that taking the waters was revived, now more for healing than for socializing. This was due to the influence of the Islamic culture. The hammam (Arabic for "spreader of warmth"), with its exquisite walled gardens, turned bathing into a more private experience often accompanied by massage and music. It was entirely different from the public routine of the Romans, involving sports and speech-making, and more akin to the spas we know today. In fact, the hammam experience that one can still enjoy throughout the modern Middle East became part of the Islamic culture, but has its roots in the ancient Mother Goddess tradition dating back to Neolithic times.

While the Roman thermae, fed by elaborate aqueduct systems, fell to ruin, natural springs still bubbled up through the earth and remained in use throughout medieval times. Their powers to cure a wide range of ailments, from impotence to rheumatism, were considered mystical. Different springs were known to be useful in treating different ills and, only later, were analyzed for their contents. There were springs valued for their temperature, flowing naturally at temperatures of more than 200 °F (93 °C). Others had a natural effervescence that soothed rheumatic pains or contained magnesium sulphate, effective as a purgative; hydrogen sulphide, a good skin treatment; or even radium, to counteract impotence. Michelangelo drank the waters from Fiuggi, a spring outside Rome, convinced that taken in large quantities, the water would break up his kidney stones.

By the 17th century, taking the waters was a fully established regime deemed essential for heath and psychological well-being. Taking the cure was a must. In France, a doctor might prescribe that a well-heeled patient—often female—drink 200 ounces of water a day from a Lalique glass. Sulphurous waters taken either as a drink or a bath were very popular in treating everything from rheumatism and diabetes to skin diseases and bad complexions, though they were not always pleasant to the senses. To create distractions, watering holes developed elaborate social and entertainment rituals, as well as creative architectural follies as meeting places, hoping to sweeten the cure.

For Europe's upper classes, going to the spas combined health seeking with social climbing. Popular spas, such as Bath in England, Karlsbad in today's Czech Republic, and Baden-Baden in Germany, saw aristocrats and the middle classes mingling freely, becoming both marriage markets and hotbeds of political activity. It was to a spa that Josephine retired in search of a treatment so that she might bear an heir to Napoleon. It was where Beethoven went to compose, George Sand and Jane Austen to write, and Chekhov to die. By the mid-19th century, when gambling was introduced, spas were the exclusive annual playground of the rich.

Spa treatments as we know them today, however, owe even more to Eastern traditions. The emphasis on achieving health through balancing mind, body, and spirit—rather than through cures to the already ailing—has its roots in Taoism. Already, by the 7th century, public baths, where observing personal hygiene was a matter of spiritual achievement, flourished in Japan. The volcanic terrain made for a tremendous variety of thermal springs, including some naturally scented by hibiscus, and others colored vermilion, emerald, or blue by minerals. The Japanese ritual of bathing, called the furo, is more like the Finnish style, where water—often salt water—is poured over embers to create steam. A tub is suspended over the steam to attain maximum heat, at least 110 °F to 126 °F (43 °C to 52 °C). Bathers, called yudedaho, or boiling octopus, did their best to stay in the water for as long as possible, perhaps three minutes, in order to achieve the perfect serenity associated with Shinto

enlightenment. Where the Romans tended to bathe in the early afternoon as a prelude to sport, the Japanese have traditionally taken their baths later, at bedtime.

Though highly sensual and often experienced nude in a nature setting, the Japanese bath experience has always been a family affair. Small groups, extreme heat, and meditation are the hallmarks of the furo and have continued to influence the way that spas are organized today. It is also true that the most memorable contemporary spas provide some of the luxury that made Roman baths such an unparalleled indulgence.

Throughout the second half of the 20th century, a numbing obsession with progress and the advancement of technology at the cost of inner awareness rendered spas almost entirely obsolete. They were seen as relics of a slower time, one more refined perhaps, but hopelessly unscientific. Today, things have changed as the medical profession only begins to fathom that natural abilities for renewal are found not only in nature, but within ourselves. And a new era of taking the waters begins.

The Retreat at Aphrodite Hills Resort, built to resemble ancient Roman thermae. Photo: Polys Pulcherios

Spas by Definition

Thermal Spas

The 50 spas profiled in this book are organized into chapter categories that best define their type. These are accepted delineations in the spa industry, and will help in your approach to visiting any of these wonderful places. The spas are looked at from three experiences: the site, the design, and the treatments. In describing spa treatments and modalities, we concentrate on the signature treatments and the more unusual services offered by each spa. You are safe to assume—even if it's not stated in the text—that most places offer the usual services of massage (such as Swedish, shiatsu, deep tissue), facials (hydrating, firming, and the like), and body treatments (scrubs, masks, and wraps).

For each section, various experts and authors introduce the different spa categories. In choosing these guides to each chapter, the single most common thread was a passion and belief in the direct benefits shared through the spa experience. We have attempted to provide examples in each category of spas that create truly memorable experiences for their guests. A brief definition of the spa categories follows.

Historically, thermal spas are the most authentic spa experiences as they are based on the basic definition of spa: *salus per aqua*, Latin for "health through water." From ancient Japanese onsens to urban European baths, thermal spas are public spaces where guests can experience the healing powers of calming waters.

Blue Lagoon thermal spa. Photo: Haukur Snorrason

Resort Spas

Wellness & Medical Spas

A resort spa is an amenity that is located within a resort complex where there is often a hotel, golf course, dining, and other such attractions. Offering services that can be purchased along with your lodging, resort spas are an exotic experience to be enjoyed during your stay away from home.

Although all spas promote well-being, wellness and medical spas are facilities that feature a medical program or have a focus on healing and supporting the welfare of their guests. Medical spas usually are staffed by doctors as well as spa therapists, and feature both medical procedures and conventional spa treatments. Extensive skincare treatments—and sometimes cosmetic surgery—are offered in a nurturing environment. Other wellness and health spas focus on holistic health, where the mind, body, and spirit are cared for as one.

COMO Shambhala at Parrot Cay resort

Skinklinic medical spa. Photo: Dan Bibb

Day Spas

Destination Spas

Offering a wide range of treatments that can be enjoyed with a smaller time commitment, day spas are a wonderful way to indulge yourself after work or on a lunch break. Responding to modern-day time constraints, day spas provide quick pick-me-ups, escapes from the mundane, and rapid relief from daily stress.

Destination spas often feature spa packages where the spa and its treatments are the main attraction, not simply an amenity. At destination spas, the whole environment is geared toward a total immersion experience and lifestyle improvement. As sanctuaries for relaxation and renewal; destination spas feature purposeful stays.

Banyan Tree Shanghai day spa

Red Mountain destination spa. Photo: Kim Cornelison

Thalasso Spas

Hotel Spas

Thalasso spas, like thermal spas, are more classical in that they offer hydrotherapy treatments. Thalasso spas use ocean water, seaweed, and algae in their preparations. From seawater tonics to injections, thalasso spas feature treatments that use the relationship between the chemistry of the human body and that of the ocean.

Hotel spas are becoming essential to hotels that want to distinguish themselves from their competition. Offering packages and day services, guests can either drop in for a quick massage or enjoy a combination of treatments. Many hotels offer in-room treatments as well. Without leaving the sanctuary of your hotel room, a specialized therapist will come to you, making the spa experience a memorable part of your stay.

Thalassa Spa features thalassotherapies. Photo: Henri Del Olmo

Spa Without Walls at The Fairmont Orchid hotel. Photo: Wally Krysciak

Thermal Spas: A Warming Trend

By Jonathan Paul de Vierville, Ph.D.

Long before contemporary culture began promoting the hot word *spa*, numerous thermal institutions served communities and entire cities as popular places for hygiene and social leisure. This practice of thermalism played a central role in personal health, civil vitality, and social regeneration. In history and in fact, the origin of all spa categories and culture begins at the hot springs and warm wells around which thermal spas emerged.

Thermal spas are all about heat. A lot of heat makes a body hot; little or no heat results in cold. Heat (hot and cold) is about energy, and thermal spas are all about energetic transference and transformation. Heat energy is exchanged from naturally heated elements of earth, water, and air to and from human bodies. Nature's elements and energies are given to humanity through forces and forms of heat: hot, warm, tepid, cool, and cold.

Regardless of the language or spelling (thermae, thermes, termas, terme, termales, termal) thermal spas provide places and processes for thermalism, the suitable and proper application of heated airs, waters, muds, peats, clays, sands, and other natural therapeutic agents on, around, in, and through the body. In rhythm and time, these thermal elemental effects and body reflexes directly and indirectly influence human hearts, minds, and souls.

Thermal spas and thermalism are the original, oldest, and authentic form of spa therapy. Earliest Stone and Bronze Age evidence of thermal spa practices are found among numerous archeological remains and artifacts uncovered at natural thermal springs, wells, baths, and pools.

Settled societies cultivated sacred rites and ritual use of thermal waters for both hygienic and religious reasons. Purity of body was as vital as purity of soul. In Delphi and Thermopylae, it was thought that Mother Earth's mineral and thermal waters emerged from the underworld and manifested the spiritual world to those who came to drink and bathe.

In the Roman world, both small and large thermal spas served as social sanctuaries. During the Republic era, small wood-covered pools called balnae served as private family baths. As Rome grew into an empire, bathing became a public rite and ritual that mingled many social and leisure benefits. The balnae turned into thermae (thermal spas), where afternoon social bathing took place in huge public watering malls akin to those built and named in honor of Titus, Domitian, Trajan, Caracalla, and Diocletian. Within these large imperial urban bathing complexes, shops, cafés, gardens, gyms, halls, schools, libraries, and theaters ringed around a central series of

Liquidrom Therme Bath. Photo: Christian Gahl

Jonathan Paul de Vierville, Ph.D., is director of the Alamo Plaza Spa at the Menger Hotel and president of the Hot Wells Institute, both in San Antonio, Texas, USA, as well as a professor of history, humanities, and global studies with a special concentration on spa cultures.

bathing rooms used for dressing and undressing, oiling, exercising, heating, sweating, scraping, scrubbing, warming, cooling, oiling again, rubbing, resting, walking, talking, meeting, and socializing.

A millennium later, enlightened Europeans rediscovered the ancient thermae and used them as models for building their *Villas Termales Citadas* (thermal spa towns) along with the addition of hotels, casinos, landscaped lakes, and nature parks.

In the Far East, the comparable social institution to thermae is Japanese onsen. Built around numerous natural flowing mineral hot springs, onsen served originally as hospital lodges for weary and wounded warriors. During peaceful times, these communal healing resorts developed into public bathing hostels where friends and families came to soak leisurely. An important ritual feature for daily Japanese thermalism is the furo, a small wooden box holding hot water (o-yu) for the afternoon bath.

East or West, the essential elements of classical thermae are not only personal hygienic hot and cold washings, but also the pleasure and leisure of social and civil bathing. Thermal spas can offer direct bodily experiences of the senses, as well as indirect experiences for one's mind, heart, and soul—in, out, and beyond time.

Our daily duties, weekly habits, and annual attitudes toward nature's thermal waters and social bathing reflect our deeper appreciation, knowledge, and understanding of meaningful living.

At the beginning, as in the end, the meaning, purpose, and importance of thermal spas are about the energies of heat: hot and cold. Thermalism includes the whole body, its flow of temperatures, time, energies, and entropy.

Thermal spas are places for personal, social, and cultural thermodynamics where nature's rhythms, elements, and waters ("The Hot Blood of Mother Earth") are central to our transformational functions, forms, and flows.

Blue Lagoon

On the southwestern tip of Iceland lays the town of Keflavik, home to a steamy wonderland known as Blue Lagoon. Naturally warm geothermal seawater pools are surrounded by lava fields and black-sand beaches, creating an otherworldly atmosphere of warmth and relaxation. In summer and in snow, bathers come to immerse themselves in the healing properties of silica, minerals, and algae, which give the water its sparkling blue hue. Blue Lagoon's proximity to the sea infuses the geothermal water that comes from boreholes of more than 6,000 feet (2,000 meters) deep with nurturing salts and minerals. The water—which is renewed every 24 hours—comprises two-thirds saltwater and one-third fresh water piped in and set at a temperature of 98 °F to 102 °F (37 °C to 39 °C). Billowing steam from the water's surface creates an almost mystical presence at the spa, which also houses an indoor pool, conference room, and restaurant.

Silica, minerals, and algae give Blue Lagoon's water its sparkling hue
Photos: Haukur Snorrason

The relaxingly modern spa facility is tucked into black lava hills, which VA Architects of Reykjavik, Iceland, uses to bond you to the unique geographic location. You are welcomed through a narrow, 650-foot (200-meter) path of tall lava walls made of some 70,000 lava pieces. The man-made lava wall continues to the interior and then back out to the site of the expansive lagoon, which bursts forward as you arrive. The double-winged building of steel, glass, and Brazilian jatoba wood overlooks broad wooden terraces and a network of curving bridges throughout the pools. Surrounding the seemingly endless lagoon are black lava outcroppings and smaller pools that radiate like apses from a cathedral. Underwater seats and benches for relaxing and treatments and an outdoor lava cave steam bath make you comfortable enough to never leave the water. If you do venture inside, you'll find a sauna with large windows overlooking the lagoon and a white-walled steam bath recalling white silica mud.

Utilizing the natural active ingredients of the lagoon—mineral salts, silica mud, and blue-green algae—Blue Lagoon's treatments aim to relax you. Boxes of white silica mud are located by the lagoon for you to apply to your face and body to cleanse, exfoliate, and firm your skin. A beautiful waterfall will give you a natural, energizing massage. Scheduled treatments take place in the open-air, 54,000-square-foot (5,000-square-meter) lagoon on specially designed benches and mattresses. Draped in blankets to keep you warm, you will experience massages and body treatments with the mud, as well as with blue-green algae that nourishes, softens, and strengthens your skin, and with mineral salts to soften, tone, and remineralize. All of this gives you and your family (massages are offered for children as young as six years old) a deep sense of balance and relaxation. Ending your day at the spa, it's recommended you engage in the 10-minute Blitz Guss, which drizzles you with fresh Icelandic water in hot, warm, and cold temperatures, making you a most satisfied creature from the beautiful Blue Lagoon.

Above left to right:
Waterfall gives a natural, vigorous massage
Rich mineral content contributes to the buoyancy of the water
White walls recall the natural tone of silica mud
Left: Decks are built out into the expansive blue water

Left to right:
Massages and treatments are conducted in the open water
You traverse the lagoon through a series of curved bridges
Steam rises from naturally heated thermal waters

Spa Bad Elster

Anointed by Saxon royalty in 1848, Bad Elster, Germany, is one of the country's oldest spa towns. The first analysis of the town's healing mineral waters was published in 1669. Situated in the land of Saxony, near Bavaria and Bohemia, this historic town is densely wooded, with hills of up to 2,100 feet (650 meters) that protect the Spa Bad Elster resort in the valley against fluctuations in temperature. Although the spa is within an historic park with buildings from the mid-19th to the early-20th centuries, the complex fell into disrepair until after Germany's reunification. Now, however, with the addition of a central bathing hall, treatment areas, and refurbishment of the historic buildings, Spa Bad Elster is visited by those wishing once again to take a cure or relax in the waters.

A glass water gate guides you from indoor to outdoor pools at Spa Bad Elster
Photos: Christian Kandzia (unless noted)

From the outside, 19th-century buildings face the street and create an interior courtyard. You enter the 186,420-square-foot (17,300-square-meter) facility through historical Albert Hall tiled in the Jugendstil style with fish and shell images, to then emerge into a modern courtyard of color and light. Stuttgart, Germany-based architects Behnisch & Partner created this striking, yet subtle, transformation. The architect's goal was for the new structure to be as transparent as possible, so as to respect the majesty of the historic buildings. Thus, glass walls, doors, beams, and ceilings encase the interior courtyard and maintain views of the sky and the wooded hills of Bad Elster. Double-glass construction and a novel heating and cooling system insulate the interior for use year round. In deliberate contrast to the older buildings, a colorful contemporary roof of moving glass louvers is dot-printed to protect bathers from sun and glare. The louvers are closed for winter and open for summer. Within the interior courtyard, several pools of varying temperatures await bathers. The buildings are square, thus the pools are round and curvy. Indoor pools are connected to the large outdoor pool by an ingenious water gate. As well, glass corridors were added to the existing buildings to further unify the space. The design encourages the relationship between inside and outside, festivity and formality, and old and new.

Like the building, you will transform from your old self into a new one by taking to the water—both externally and internally. All pools are stocked with water from the medicinal mineral springs, and there are private tubs in the treatment areas so you can alter the temperature and mineral content. Spa Bad Elster offers drinking cures that claim to be curative against metabolic, kidney, and bladder disorders. In addition to the mineral baths that help overall disease prevention, moor mud baths and packs aid in arthritis and muscle pain. Steam rooms, several saunas, and massage treatments are available. Doctors of water therapy are on hand to give you guidance and personalized advice on building immunity, curing ailments, rebuilding agility, and attaining overall rejuvenation, so that you will emerge more transparent and unified than ever.

Above left to right:
Huge windows maintain a connection between indoors and out
The spa is set in the valley of wooded hills
Glass corridors unite disparate historic buildings. Photo: Martin Schodder
Left: Outdoor pool is filled with healing mineral water. Photo: Martin Schodder

Above: Old forms contrast with new
Left: Round pools play counterpoint to the square
interior courtyard structure

Liquidrom Therme Bath

Harking back to the historical, all-encompassing definition of thermae, Liquidrom Therme Bath in Berlin, Germany, is a combination of thermal bath, bar, and nightclub, giving you the necessary human connection with water within a vibrant governmental and cultural center. Berlin itself has a strong association with water, sporting two large and six small rivers, 10 canals, 50 large lakes, and 100 small lakes. So it's appropriate that Berlin be host to a spa based on the idea of "water dreaming"—a melding of thermal waters, relaxing sounds, and intriguing imagery.

Sculptural forms create an embracing experience at Liquidrom Therme Bath
Photo: Linda Troeller

Just 10 minutes from Potsdamer Platz is the Tempodrom, a multimedia center, home to two performance arenas and Liquidrom. Architect von Gerkan, Marg and Partner of Hamburg created Tempodrom, with its elaborate, tent-like exterior, as well as the sophisticated interiors of Liquidrom spa, which are spare and geometric. Limited to a muted palette of color and materials, most walls are finished with refined concrete. Floors and walls in wet and bathing areas are green-gray natural stone, and wood details are of untreated red cedar. Changing rooms, baths, and the bar are based on strong orthogonal principles. In beautiful contrast, the Grotto is a round, 400-square-foot (35-square-meter) warm saline pool in a dramatic domed interior with graceful curved arches.

The centerpiece of Liquidrom, the Grotto, is where the magic happens, courtesy of Liquid Sound. A pioneer of Balneo-Sono-Color-Relaxation, Liquid Sound employs colored light, music, and nature sounds to instill deep inner tranquillity. Equipped with 12 underwater speakers, the pool may transmit music from classical to techno, or recordings of marine animal sounds (it was the sound of whales communicating in the water that inspired Liquid Sound's creation). As you float in the body-temperature salt water with your ears below the surface, you experience hearing multi-dimensionally, through all parts of your body. Concurrently, images, colors, and films are projected onto the smooth concrete surfaces for a total sensory experience. The Grotto holds up to 50 floaters—optionally in the nude—making the experience communal as well. You may easily go from Grotto to bar and back, or enjoy saunas, steam rooms, cold plunge pool, and outdoor Japanese-inspired hot pool. Treatments include massage, structural body work, the Beauty Face Massage combination of holistic and ayurvedic techniques, and Energetic Trance Warm Oil Massage. Aqua Wellness Bodywork gives you massage and stretching in the thermal pool. For dry sound experiences, there are sound rooms and chairs, and the OM Room, which reacts to your presence as you make or hear planetary sounds. Moonlight streams through the Grotto's oculus as the only illumination needed for special full-moon live concerts that give you an otherworldly experience.

Minimalist interiors use a limited materials palette. Photo: Christian Gahl

Above: Rich, red cedar wood gives warmth to fine-grain concrete. Photo: Christian Gahl
Top right: Outdoor hot pool is based on Japanese onsen. Photo: Linda Troeller
Bottom right: Liquidrom's bar is a busy social spot. Photo: Linda Troeller

 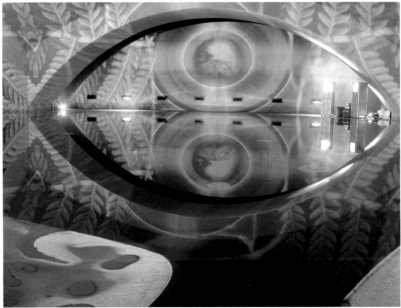 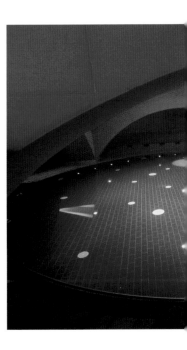

Left to right:
Color washes over concrete and water
Projected images and music inspire "water dreaming"
Images play perception games with the space

Sweeping curves give lightness to concrete
You experience Aqua Wellness in the body-temperature water
Photos: Linda Troeller

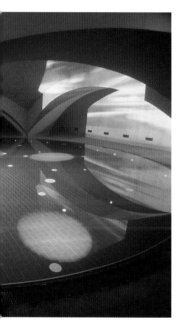 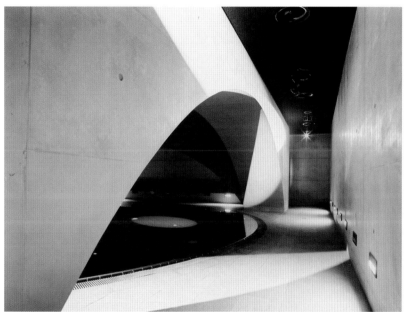 

Takaragawa Onsen

More than 1,000 years old, the Japanese art of bathing is performed beautifully at Takaragawa Onsen in the Gumma province of Japan. The country boasts some 2,000 natural hot springs (or onsen) resulting from the abundance of volcanoes on the islands. The strong local custom of communal bathing in mineral hot springs originated with the aristocracy, then evolved through the centuries to include all classes. Just west of Tokyo, Takaragawa is largely thought of as Japan's leading outdoor bath, and is visited year-round. Nestled in a pine forest high in the mountains, the stunning scenery changes with the seasons, from snowy winter to cherry blossoms in spring, green summer, and colorful autumn.

The steamy water at Takaragawa Onsen is rich with minerals
Photos: courtesy Takaragawa Onsen

When visiting, you may come for the day, or stay in a Japanese inn (ryokan) beautifully appointed with traditional tatami mats, shoji screens, and lanterns. The ryokan overlooks a mountain river that snakes through the property. Sheltered under a huge thatched roof, guest rooms embrace the forest, not only with lush views, but also with design details of tall, natural logs with sculptural qualities. Originally built in the mid-1950s, the guest rooms maintain their traditional looks, although the lobby, restaurants, and shop employ highly contemporary designs. To the get to the open-air baths (rotemburo) from the inn, you cross a bamboo bridge, passing koi ponds and landscaped gardens along the way. A series of roofed structures within the waters offers shelter and shade.

Open wood hut changing rooms allow you to shed your clothes—and inhibitions—as the custom is to bathe *au naturel* in the communal baths, as well as in separate men's and women's baths. Be aware, however, that the word "bathe" is misleading, as onsen are strictly for soaking up the healing powers of the warm, mineral-rich water. You are expected to give yourself a good soap scrub first, followed by a thorough rinse, as there are no suds allowed in the onsen. Takaragawa's rocky banks of the river form the amorphously shaped rotemburo that are further ringed with rock formations, stone lanterns, and statues. Hot mineral water from a subterranean source and warm rocks in the water maintain the heat. Though the outdoor baths are used often in winter months, you may also partake of those indoor— if you can bear to be away from the rushing river water and natural setting for even a moment.

Above: Onsen mesh with natural waters, with little distinction
Right: Contemporary design mixes with traditional touches
Far right: Rocky river banks give shape to the onsen

Above: Rocky outcroppings are natural seating areas
Right: Roofed structures give shade and shelter

Above: You can experience onsen year-round
Right: A natural river rushes through the property
Opposite: Lush landscaping surrounds the pools

Thermae Bath Spa

It's ironic that in a town called Bath, no one has been allowed to use the legendary waters from the late 1970s until now. The town of Bath, England—the United Kingdom's only natural hot springs site—is open to bathers once again, and in great style at Thermae Bath Spa. The walled city of Bath has been hailed for its healing springs since Celtic times. Water from these springs is believed to have fallen as rain some 10,000 years ago, and then sank to a depth of about 1.25 miles (2 kilometers) below the earth's surface. It was then heated by high-temperature rocks before rising back up through a break in the limestone that lies beneath the city. But when the 113 °F (45 °C) water stopped flowing, the buildings went into stark disrepair and the town suffered. Named a World Heritage City, the government helped in the late 1990s by partly financing the restoration of five historic buildings and the design of a new one for Thermae Bath Spa. New boreholes were made to ensure freshness, and the waters were brought back to Bath.

Round pods give space-age appeal to the steam floor at Thermae Bath Spa
Photo: Edmond Sumner

The feelings of history and renewal are evident in the architecture by Nicholas Grimshaw & Partners with conservation architect Donald Insall Associates, both of London. Traditional buildings of stone, granite, and timber are combined with contemporary elements of glass and concrete. The New Royal Bath is a stone cube set within glass, a stark contrast to the historic Cross Bath, Hot Bath, and Hetling Building. Four of the buildings in the complex are interlinked on one side of Bath Street, while the Cross Bath and Hetling Building stand discretely on the other side of the street. The interplay between new and old is heightened by the liberal use of glass to connect the spaces and bring in light. Natural light in the day and architectural lighting in the evening create transparency and reflection and enhance the relationships between light and shade, and solid and void. A limited range of simple geometric forms brings a sense of cohesion to the complex. A circular stone tower with porthole-like windows makes a bold street statement, and is then echoed in the interior steam rooms, whose circular pods have a space-age feeling.

A year-round, open-air rooftop pool at the New Royal Bath gives you a beautiful view of the historic skyline and green hills surrounding Bath. Air jets perform relaxing neck massage in the water, which is pumped from nearby Hetling, Cross, and Kings Springs. Essential oils of eucalyptus, mint, lavender, pine, and jasmine infuse the healthful air on the steam floor, which bathes you in light as well as aromatic vapors. Waterfall showers are also enhanced with fiber optic lighting. Hot Bath, originally designed by John Wood the Younger in the 18th century, offers watsu treatments, Moroccan Mud Wraps, and Aromatherapy Cocoons, as well as the Alpine Hay Chamber, where soothing herbs are released into the atmosphere. An open-air thermal bath awaits you at Cross Bath, where you can enjoy a variety of dry flotation treatments—passive immersions on warmed cushions of water. You experience no direct contact with the water, yet feel the effects of movement. Goat's milk, aloe vera, and macadamia, jojoba, and grapeseed oils infuse your Cleopatra Bath, giving new meaning to an old custom.

Top left: Herbal and light infusions enhance your steam experience. Photo: Nick Smith
Top right: Natural and artificial lighting sets many moods. Photo: Nick Smith
Above: Year-round rooftop pool overlooks skyline and hills of Bath. Photo: Edmond Sumner

Top right: A new glass roof encloses the historic Hot Bath. Photo: Edmond Sumner
Bottom right: Historic buildings are linked with a new structure. Photo: Edmond Sumner

Therme Vals

The dramatic Therme Vals—a contemporary take on the most ancient of spa types—is found in Graubünden, Switzerland, a small canton in a basin-shaped valley. The town had fallen on hard times, with not much to claim, except for the numbers of young people and jobs that were fleeing for the larger cities. Banding together, the community revived an old hotel and brought thermal healing back to the area, which had been a spa town since 1893. Set 4,000 feet (1,200 meters) above sea level is St. Peter's spring, which delivers 86 °F (30 °C) water for the experience of bathing and relaxing in thermal warmth. The hotel, which is a pastiche of old and new appointments, has some 120 rooms outfitted with modern furniture and Oriental rugs. Rather than flee, visitors now flock to Graubünden to enjoy the spring grotto, scented flower pool, drink grotto with spring water, indoor and outdoor pools, steam rock, sweat bath rock, fire pool of 107.5 °F (42 °C), and 57 °F (14 °C) ice pool.

Minimalist loungers are place in a frame overlooking the landscape at Therme Vals
Photo: Tim Griffith

Reached by an underground passage from the hotel, the spa appears as a grass-covered stone object that seems to have emerged from the mountain. The work of Swiss architect Peter Zumthor, Therme Vals is a visual and visceral dance of density and void, light and dark. Seemingly hollowed out from the mountain, the complex of interconnected open and closed geometric caves and caverns is made from 60,000 Valser quartzite slabs from stone quarries further up the valley. The deep, graphite-colored stone is not mere facing, but is wholly structural. Narrow slits where walls seem to not quite touch each other emit dramatic slivers of light, creating a changing tableau throughout the day. Square skylights are punched into the ceiling over the baths for additional dramatic lighting effects. A broad patio in between two wings of the structure is lined with minimalist lounge chairs facing the majestic Swiss mountains. The severe shapes emphasize the architect's avoidance of natural form, but are created with natural materials, setting up an inherent—and delightful—contradiction.

The intention of Therme Vals is the silent experience of bathing and relaxing in differing temperatures of water. It is meant as a personal and elemental experience between you, the water, and the stone of Vals. In addition to the vast indoor and outdoor thermal baths, you may partake in Massage Baths with little jets of water massaging you with sea salt, kelp, or Caribbean oils. Weekly regimes focus on bathing, slimming, thalasso pampering, and stress reduction. Hot and cold thalasso therapies employ kelp, sea salt, and mint, while Warm Fen-Pack mud treatments are recommended preludes to massages. Milk and fruit acids regenerate, repair, and activate your skin in a facial influenced by the ancient recipe of Cleopatra's milk bath. Based on traditional Chinese medicine, Chi Yang is an acupressure massage with pure oils and 22-carat gold particles, bringing you in touch with the bountiful treasures of the mountains.

Vast thermal pool is accented by square skylights. Photo: Tim Griffith

Top: Narrow slits of light dance upon the stone. Photo: Henry Pierre Schultz
Bottom: Water, light, and stone are in constant interplay. Photo: Tim Griffith
Right: Local quartzite forms the structure of interlinking caves and caverns. Photo: Henry Pierre Schultz

Resort Spas: Resorting to Well-Being by Bernard Burt

In an era when spas define the very nature of resorts, new design concepts are redefining how we spa. Blending fantasy and reality, cross-cultural experiences in tropical gardens or mountain retreats feature indigenous treatments with herbs, seaweed, mud, and floral lotions.

Like the fashion industry, spas reflect our times. It's not about in-your-face opulence, but creating and maintaining the dream of beauty and wellness. The hot trend is cross-cultural fusion, created by a wave of Asian resorts and cosmetics companies. Oriental fantasies take many forms, from facials to bodywork. Experiencing the real thing used to mean travel to exotic resorts in Thailand, Malaysia, and scattered islands of the Pacific. But you can now find Balinese lulur or Indian ayurvedic treatments across North America and Europe. Watsu, a waterborne form of shiatsu massage, appears at Amelia Island resort in Florida. Yoga, once thought to be an Indian cult exercise, draws sophisticated travelers to Parrot Cay in the Turks and Caicos Islands, as well as to a palace hidden in the Himalayas. Aromatherapy in a Mexican garden by the sea in Baja California provides relaxation for body, mind, and spirit.

Serendipity by design, some call it. Infinity pools flow in Mexico and Marrakech as well as Evian and Baden-Baden. Beautiful baths are expected in California or France. But soaking in a traditional steeping tub set in the tropical gardens of Indonesia or the Seychelles transports you to a new level of paradise.

Because every experience is different, no two spas are alike. Defining the difference has been a decades-long journey for me, during which I've spanned many parts of the globe. Marked by explosive growth, spas saw a quantum shift in the new millennium: more men and families sample spa services, while typical spa-goers are younger. Resorts responded with couples' massage, mother–daughter weeks, and programs that fit today's schedules. Staying fit, if polls are to be believed, is less important than luxurious pampering. "One should always have fun," says interior designer Clodagh. Travel agent Jenni Lipa sees resort spas filling a global need for human touch. Enjoying the best of both worlds, you can combine spa and sports, enjoy elegant cuisine without dieting, and indulge in treatments that suit your lifestyle.

COMO Shambhala at Parrot Cay. Photo: courtesy Parrot Cay

Bernard Burt is co-author of *100 Best Spas of the World* (Globe-Pequot Press) and founding director of the International Spa Association (ISPA).

Creating a resort where every element melds with the spa is increasingly difficult in today's world of hotel brand marketing. The real challenge "is to recognize that we are caregivers, and our mission is to create a nurturing and supportive environment that has the potential of making a difference in the lives of others," says Karen Korpi, vice president for spa development and operations for the Ritz-Carlton Hotel Company.

Never before have there been so many choices. The growth rate for resort spas continued in the aftermath of the events of September 11th, perhaps because we need safe places to rejuvenate and re-create ourselves, to cocoon in a romantic environment. *Joie de vivre*—the joy of living—is what distinguishes this new breed of resort spa. Forget bland rooms and decor; expect to be wowed by the look and feeling of a place like no other. Designers draw on native cultures, just as therapists find inspiration in traditional healing. Past and present meet in a seamless experience that leaves you feeling it's been the best vacation of a lifetime.

Island Spa at Kuda Huraa

Your journey to an island paradise begins immediately, as you board a dhoni—a native boat—to reach the private island that houses the Island Spa at Kuda Huraa. Occupying the entire island, the spa is part of the Four Seasons Resort Maldives at Kuda Huraa, situated on the North Malé Atoll of the Republic of Maldives. Sparkling turquoise waters surround the white-sand beaches of Kuda Huraa. Ingeniously extending its property, the Four Seasons created a series of bungalow accommodations reaching out to the tiny Reef Island and beyond that have the complete feeling of floating upon the water (because they are!). There's even a man-made ocean, with an enormous pool, whose infinity edge blends the pool and ocean waters.

Board the native boat—a dhoni—to begin your journey to Island Spa at Kuda Huraa
Photos: Peter Mealin

Calling on design influences from India and Morocco, Western Australia-based Grounds Kent Architects and interior designer Hinke Zieck create a warm atmosphere of repose and relaxation. Within a tent of billowing white cloth, a welcoming, circular spa reception area greets you with large pillows piled on comfortable seating areas. Blue tones mimicking the scenic ocean complement the sandy white tones of the reception desk and walls. Display cabinets shaped like the dhoni boats are filled with souvenirs of your experience. Five thatched-roof, jalousie-walled treatment pavilions line the island and hover over the brilliant ocean. Massage tables are located over floor cut-outs so you gaze at the blue depths of the Indian Ocean while nestled in the face cradle. Each pavilion is equipped with bathing area, garden courtyard, open-air shower, and meditation platform—all in discreet privacy. Bungalows replicate the spa atmosphere with thatched roofs, white walls, blue accents, private decks, and pools.

Healing elements of the sea are emphasized in the selection of treatments from India, Thailand, and Indonesia. Ayurvedic healing is a focus here. The 5,000-year-old healing "science of life" (*ayu* means life; *vedic* is knowledge, in Sanskrit) prominently features the slow dripping of herbal oils onto various parts of your body. Oils are also used for Indian and Balinese massages, whereas traditional Thai massage is performed wearing a soft cotton Siam outfit. Body treatments use herbal, seaweed, and tropical garden ingredients to detoxify, and sea salts, blended herbs, and seeds for exfoliation. In the pavilion equipped with the Vichy shower you can experience the Maldivian Monsoon Ritual, beginning with a sandalwood body scrub rinsed by the deluge—a veritable monsoon rain—from the Vichy shower. Followed by a warm herbal oil massage and then steam bath, this signature treatment concludes with frankincense-sandalwood body lotion application, which makes your journey complete.

Left: A sprawling blue-tiled pool visually blends into the sea
Right: Guest rooms hover above the Indian Ocean

Guest suite deck leads out to the beach

Spa at Amelia Island Plantation

Beautiful birds soar through Amelia Island, the southern-most of the Atlantic barrier islands, 30 miles (48 kilometers) north of Jacksonville, Florida, USA. The Spa at Amelia Island Plantation is nestled within lagoons, a bird sanctuary, and towering majestic trees. The eco-sensitive island is home to sweetwater oaks and more than 80 species of birds. You are bound to see pelicans fly by, or ospreys, egrets, red-tailed hawks, spoonbills, sandpipers, and warblers. Long bridges and walkways connect various buildings, and give you the feeling of traipsing lightly upon such precious land. The spa complex respects Amelia Island's preservationist philosophy by maintaining a delicate balance between nature and the built environment. Host to a variety of wild and plant life, Amelia is in synch with her new role of hosting humans seeking a sybaritic experience.

Spa at Amelia Island Plantation is set within an eco-sensitive landscape. Photo: Eric Laignel

Inspired and informed by the natural beauty of Amelia, New York City-based Robert D. Henry Architects envisioned an eco-sensitive facility to pay homage to the pristine, unspoiled atmosphere of this premier destination. Architecturally, Henry draws on the vernacular of the Old South, while using an earthy palette and local materials to set the facility in harmony with nature. The design is based on an episodic journey, which you start in the soaring lobby space that stretches skyward as light filters through a two-story forest of exposed timber lattice. Continuing along the spa journey, you come upon a meditation garden, the epicenter of the spa. Twin treatment buildings take a giant step back to allow an infill of sky in a gesture that results in the formation of a magnificent outdoor room that terraces down to a lagoon. From the meditation garden, you gain access to the footbridge that spans over the lagoon to a tiny speck of an island. The island—anchored by two majestic 5-foot (1.5-meter) diameter, 80-year-old sweetwater oaks draped in Spanish moss—is where the watsu pavilion is sited.

The spa and retail village include 25 treatment rooms and full salon and spa shop for both day and resort visitors. Signature services revolve around water, and include ionotherapy, which combats fatigue by the absorption of negative ions through mineral-infused waters and seaweed. Water-based treatments reaffirm your connection to the eco-sensitive island experience and your journey to the watsu pool connects you back with nature. Watsu (whose name is derived from the words *water* and *shiatsu*) is a massage method that practices Zen shiatsu in waters close to body temperature. The buoyancy of the water takes the weight off your vertebrae and you become as sinuous as a piece of seaweed floating in a peaceful lagoon.

Above: The Southern design is maintained in every corner of the spa. Photo: Eric Laignel
Left: As does the island itself, you float in the water during watsu. Photo: Dan Bibb
Opposite left: Relaxation lounge is soft and serene. Photo: Dan Bibb
Opposite right: Towering timbers welcome you to the spa. Photo: Dan Bibb

Top left to right:
Elevated pathways lead you across the lagoon from one building to another. Photo: Dan Bibb
Southern-style architecture sets a relaxed mood. Photo: Dan Bibb
Rhythmic pattern of shutters allows air to flow, while keeping hot sun at bay. Photo: Eric Laignel
Above: Decades-old trees and vegetation dictated the arrangement of buildings on the site. Photo: Dan Bibb

Banyan Tree Bintan

Like the broad, sheltering boughs of its namesake, Banyan Tree welcomes you to Bintan, Indonesia, gateway to the Riau Archipelago. The resort is situated on a secluded bay on the northwestern tip of the island. Part of the Banyan Tree philosophy—and what has given it a prominent name in eco-tourism—is to maintain the natural setting of its locales. Thus, the island's rugged coastline, with its dramatic rock formations, is preserved by designing the buildings on stilts. This also gives you exceptional views of the South China Sea from the 72 elevated villas. On the grounds are two pools—one formed around ancient rocks and shaded by trees, and the other overlooking the beach. Plus, each villa either has a private spa tub or pool.

Ancient rocks and shade trees surround the rock pool at Banyan Tree Bintan
Photos: courtesy Banyan Tree Hotels & Resorts

Architrave Design and Planning of Singapore, a division of Banyan Tree, created the buildings, which are a fusion of traditional Balinese, Javanese, and Thai architectures. The designers insisted on using only local materials, such as granite, alang-alang grass for thatched roofs, and lava stone. Whitewashed walls are accented by carved wood and stone detailing. Interiors by H.L. Lim & Associates of Singapore are contemporary in style, using a limited palette of finishes. Given that the natural beauty of the island was left largely undisturbed by the buildings, no additional landscaping was necessary. Indeed, the lush tropical trees and vegetation dictated the planning of all buildings, as well as pools. As you approach the spa, a centuries-old tree greets you at the entrance. The spa itself is designed to take full advantage of the natural location, setting the stage for the transformational treatments you'll experience. Full-height windows abound to afford views of the calming sea.

The tropical garden spa experience envelops you in exotic botanical ingredients and Asian treatments. The spa offers numerous packages of grouped treatments, all beginning with a footbath, and leading into a variety of scrubs, massages, facials, and body treatments. Spa therapists attend the Banyan Tree Spa Academy, where they log 430 hours of training in every treatment aspect, from human anatomy and pressure points, to harvesting herbs for aromatic treatments. The Banyan Massage—a combination of Eastern and Western techniques—features herbal pouches filled with lemongrass, cloves, and coriander for aromatic relaxation. The spa's Harmony Massage treats you to two therapists working simultaneously on either side of the body, ending with your head and feet massaged at the same time. Banyan Tree's Tropical Rainmist treatments combine steam and rain showers with luscious body treatments inspired by the lush surroundings.

Top: Villas built on stilts preserve the natural landscape of Bintan

Above: An organic, pond-like shape forms the beach pool

Opposite: Sculptures and a variety of seating arrangements accent this pool villa

The Retreat at Aphrodite Hills Resort

The Goddess of Wisdom guides you through The Retreat at Aphrodite Hills Resort, where you experience the ancient richness of Cyprus. The elevated site overlooks the waves of the Mediterranean Sea, from which Aphrodite was (purportedly) born. Infinity pools hover over the blue water and lush landscape, which mirrors the herb, flower, and citrus gardens that grace the resort itself. Set within monastic, stone buildings, The Retreat stresses your personal journey, looking toward the future on the foundations of the past. Cyprus' setting within the blue waters of the Mediterranean inspired the abounding water on the grounds of Aphrodite Hills. Dancing fountains maintain the constant soothing sound of water.

Vegetation surrounding The Retreat at Aphrodite Hills Resort is inspiration for treatments
Photos: Polys Pulcherios

Water, too, is the basis of the thermae, which informs the design by the London office of architect Wimberly Allison Tong & Goo and interior designer HBA/Hirsch Bedner Associates; Cyprus-based Yiannos Anastasiou Architects coordinated with both firms. Starting with the idea of a monastery built on ruins of Roman thermae, The Retreat is constructed around a colonnaded central courtyard with spacious, galleried hallways. Local stone, tile mosaics, and sea views at every turn bring you back to the mythological site. The thermae—the centerpiece of classical and historical Greco-Roman bathing rituals of cleansing and relaxation—are organized around a stone atrium, which allows light to penetrate to the lower bath areas. Private massage treatment rooms on the upper level are bathed with more light and air, and boast access to the outdoor courtyard and upper-level pool. Massage pavilions set within the fragrant herb and flower gardens bring you in touch with the natural elements.

Keeping with ancient traditions, you can take a journey through a sequence of rooms for a truly transformational experience. Start with the relaxing tepidarium, a mild heat room with heated loungers overlooking the garden, then increase the temperature and humidity in the caldarium to benefit your respiratory system and skin. Humidity decreases, but things get even hotter for ultimate detoxifying in the laconium, which is then countered by circulation-stimulating cooling showers at the frigidarium. The Retreat's signature Bathing Rituals combine guided use of the thermae with massage and body treatments based on local resources, such as olives, rosewater, and almond, to make you feel like a true god or goddess.

Left to right:
Refined versions of stone and columns grace the spa waiting areas
The feature olive tree welcomes you to your bathing journey
The Retreat is designed to resemble a monastery built on ruins of ancient Roman thermae

Left: The essences of olives, rosewater, and almonds swathe you in comfort and relaxation
Above: The mosaic-lined pool visually blends with the Mediterranean Sea

Amanjena Health and Beauty Center

Amanjena means "peaceful paradise," which is just what this oasis in Marrakech, Morocco, promises you. Its earthen walls rise among date palms and old olive trees on land that was for centuries agricultural. Locating Amanjena Health and Beauty Center around a bassin—traditionally an irrigation holding pool—emphasizes the site's agrarian history, while bringing it to the present day. Now, the bassin's water is used to nourish olive, palm, and citrus trees as well as bountiful flowers. Marrakech, known as the Red City, is reflected in the deep sandstone pink buildings housing 34 pavilions and six duplex townhouses, or maisons. The pavilion courtyard affords you views of the olive groves and golf course. Maisons each have their own pool, while two boast large gardens with fountains and fireplaces.

The sprawling Amanjena Health and Beauty Center is set within a traditional bassin
Photos: courtesy AmanResorts

Paris-based architect Design Realization leans heavily on formal Moroccan architecture and motifs. The articulated green clay rooflines and dusty-pink walls of pavilions, villas, and maisons are reflected in the bassin. Colonnades of distinctive Moroccan arches create processionals through the resort's public areas, including open courtyards with fountains that keep the sound of flowing water constant. The importance of water is manifested in the numerous reflecting pools, as well as in the large swimming pool lined in hand-cut green tiles. A feeling of coolness in the desert climate is maintained by the tiled floors and wall insets, which are complemented by Arabic carpets, ceiling lanterns, and flowing drapery. Exquisite detailing is seen in the hand-carved wood screens and doors, traditional tile work, and 80 onyx columns that grace The Moroccan, a restaurant featuring innovative approaches to local cuisine.

Central to Moroccan life is the hammam, so it's no surprise that your experience at this peaceful paradise revolves around the traditional steam bath. Each of two facilities (separate for men and women) features a stepped, two-chamber room with beautiful tiled walls and embracing arches. From the glassed-in whirlpools, you gaze out onto the fountain courtyards. Your traditional Moroccan Treatment starts with a wash with black soap made from olive residue, which is rinsed by buckets of warm water. Hand and feet pumice follow, along with a body scrub with hammam glove. More indigenous ingredients—Moroccan clay, lavender, rosewater, dried plants, and spices—are rubbed on your entire body. Finish with mint tea and a steam, and you have immersed yourself in the ultimate Moroccan paradise.

Above: Two-chamber resting room is exquisitely detailed
Left: Colors of Marrakech—the Red City—influence the design

Above: Whirlpools look out onto the fountain courtyards
Right: Hot reds and cool greens surround treatment areas

COMO Shambhala at Parrot Cay

Your own private island awaits at Parrot Cay, one of the eight inhabited Turks and Caicos Islands in the British West Indies (there are more than 40 smaller cays). This 1,000-acre (404-hectare) island is a natural wetlands habitat with white sandy beaches, bright turquoise water, and myriad tropical birds. Here, luxury and holistic healing coexist, with 66 private villas, some with up to three bedrooms and their own swimming pools and beachfront. Rooms are situated along the beach, over the garden, or on an extra-exclusive area called Rocky Point.

Tiki hut at COMO Shambhala at Parrot Cay provides shade and relaxation
Photos: courtesy Parrot Cay

The resort's design is decidedly low-key, with white-walled, timber-clad, scenery-hugging villas by architect Rothermel Cooke Smith, based on Providenciales, the largest island in Turks and Caicos. Summery interiors by London's United Designers feature antique and contemporary teak furniture from famed Bali-based manufacturer Warisan, accented with diaphanous white fabrics. That breezy, light feeling continues at COMO Shambhala, Parrot Cay's center of peace and harmony. The four buildings comprising the yoga-oriented spa are built of weathered pine on wooden platforms over wetlands and cooled by island wafts. Resembling an ancient temple, it is a place of holy stillness, which is meant to infuse you with the sense of health and well-being. The main building has treatment rooms, dining, sauna, steam, and an infinity pool that seemingly blends into the ocean. For the ultimate in luxury and privacy, you can use the spa cottage, which is reserved for couples' treatments.

Yoga, Pilates, tai chi, and movement are featured here—with occasional week-long yoga retreats with masters from throughout the world. Imported oils, herbs, spices, and flowers highlight the Asian-style treatments. Eastern massages include tui na, based on the Chinese healing art using pushing (tui) and grasping (na); Thai massage, often described as "passive yoga"; and Shambhala Massage with pure essential oils that stimulate your lymphatic system. For the total experience, there's the Parrot Cay Bath, a cleansing treatment that starts with a signature salt scrub infused with essential oils, macadamia oil, and oat bran, and concludes with the Shambhala Massage. Parrot Cay's activities aim to connect you to your own private oasis in your soul.

Opposite: Parrot Cay is a 1,000-acre (404-hectare) island in the sparkling seas of the West Indies

Top left: Yoga pavilions resemble ancient temples
Bottom left: Diaphanous white fabrics and natural teak define the interiors
Top: The Parrot Cay Bath includes body scrub and massage
Bottom: Instructors from throughout the world hold yoga workshops at COMO Shambhala

Nemacolin Woodlands Resort and Spa

A woodland wonderland in the mountains of Farmington, Pennsylvania, USA, Nemacolin Woodlands Resort and Spa is a full-service resort. Its 2,800 acres (1,133 hectares) offer you two PGA golf courses, equestrian center, miniature golf, tennis courts, ski slopes, shooting academy, shopping arcades, conference center, ballroom, and private airfield. Named after the native Delaware Indian chief who carved a trail through the Laurel Highlands in 1740, Nemacolin became popular as a resort town in the 1930s. Its most famous family—the Kaufmanns—built Frank Lloyd Wright's Fallingwater nearby. This large resort includes 335 guest rooms.

Pools reflect the lush landscaping surrounding Nemacolin Woodlands Resort and Spa
Photos: Daniel Aubrey

Taking its cue from the natural forests, the Woodlands Spa is both rustic and Zen-like in its design. Burt Hill Kosar Rittleman Associates of Pittsburgh, PA, is responsible for the architecture, while the carefully appointed spa and restaurant interiors, as well as the surrounding landscape, are by Clodagh Design International of New York City. Natural light abounds in the spaces, which use indigenous materials to reconfirm the sense of place and stress eco-friendliness. Relying on the ancient Chinese philosophy of feng shui, the design works in harmony with the earth's environment and uses the basic elements of wood, fire, earth, metal, and water. You experience these elements upon arrival to the building, which is set within lush landscaping that includes an aromatherapy garden, birch groves, Irish moss garden, trellises adorned with trumpet vines and wisteria, and reflecting pools. Snaking through the gardens is an 80-foot (24-meter) moat over which you traverse a wooden bridge, leading you into the spa building, and literally guiding you from one world to the other. Beyond the cast-bronze entry doors, the 32,000-square-foot (2,975-square-meter) spa features 28 private therapy rooms, herbal Krauter baths, Swiss shower, mineral pool, salon, indoor and outdoor pools, and water path (a rarity in the United States). The indoor–outdoor design concept continues in the treatment rooms, which sport warm wooden planks on walls, combined with cool, clean stainless steel. The whirlpool areas are lined in granite evocative of moss and earth on a woodland path. Expressive "leaf" lamps of resin and metal decorate the ceiling over the interior swimming pool pavilion, and an abundance of glass and light leaves it visually open to the sky.

The granite water path is the signature treatment at Nemacolin. With the guidance of a therapist, you walk in two pebble-lined, knee-high troughs filled with mineral water, one cold and one hot. Alternating temperatures stimulates circulation and improves blood and lymph flow. Your hot/cold experience continues with a warm shower followed by soak with therapeutic thermal mineral salts from the Sarvar Springs of Hungary, and ends with a cool Swiss shower. Also popular are the hot-stone treatments—massage and pedicure—that carry on the outdoors theme of the spa. Woodlands Hot Stone Shirodhara combines hot-stone massage, reiki, and ayurvedic shirodhara. Body services use natural ingredients of protein-rich spirulina, mineral-laced moor mud, and calming chamomile. Seasons, the spa restaurant, offers "Conscious Paleolithic Cuisine," which features regional and local ingredients combined to promote optimum vitality.

Left: Mineral bath tubs are lined with granite resembling moss and earth
Opposite bottom: Treatment rooms are serene with natural wood planks and cool stainless steel

Top left: Natural, eco-sensitive materials
are used throughout
Top right: Gaia is in the details: a bud vase
is integrated into the wall

Vigilius Mountain Resort

Tucked discreetly into the Tyrolian Dolomite mountains, Vigilius Mountain Resort is a true merging of nature and architecture. The remote 3.5-acre (1.4-hectare) site in Lana, Italy, is reachable only by cable car or foot up the 4,920-foot (1,500-meter) mountain. The beautiful expanse of the mountain inspires Vigilius' mission of holistic health and environmental conservation. Indeed, the Vigiljoch Mountain landscape is not just thought of as the backdrop, but as the essence of the place. The pristine stillness outside is meant to mirror a renewed spirit inside you. It's a spot that removes you from daily bothers, and delivers you to a more elemental realm.

Indoor pool at Vigilius Mountain Resort leads seamlessly to outdoor whirlpool on terrace
Photo: Thierry Malty

In keeping with the connection to the landscape, Milan-based architect Matteo Thun created Vigilius to emphasize the natural site. The low-lying building is designed with local materials, such as larch pine wood, silver quartz, and raw clay. These materials, used in their natural states, comprise the very soothing contemporary architecture. The feeling of a private tree house emerges from the network of larch shade-giving slats encasing the building and a natural sod roof on top. Six suites and 35 guest rooms are colored by the dawn or sunset, due to the siting of the building. Rooms are paneled in warm-toned wood and feature a clay-covered, heated partition between the bed and bath areas. Bright spots of orange enliven the rooms. The two-level spa continues the minimal feeling with a variety of treatment rooms, sauna, steam, and movement room, all open to terraces beyond the wooden slats. Highlights include the huge outdoor Paradise Garden and terrace and the dramatic indoor pool, which overlooks the valley through expansive glass.

Waters from Vigiljoch Mountain are tapped for both drinking and bathing cures. The waters are used in hydrotherapies, such as one with a Manual Detoxification Massage to stimulate the elimination of toxins in your body. Combining relaxation and beauty is the Shiatsu Wash and Style, including a luxurious shampoo on the shiatsu shampoo bed, a scalp massage, then hair style. Exclusive to the spa is its own Apple Honey Body Polish, which exfoliates your skin with a warm combination of honey, apple, and polenta. A traditional treatment in South Tyrol, the Hay Bath is well known for its cleansing and detoxifying effects, as well as for the reduction of pain and arthritis. Fermented hay from the high mountain is placed on your body. You are then lowered into a warm suspension bath of 104 °F (40 °C), forever merging your soul with the land around you.

Top: Low-lying building blends into nature. Photo: Christine Schaum
Above: You gaze out to the Tyrolian landscape from the yoga studio. Photo: Christine Schaum

Top left: A network of wooden slats encases the building. Photo: Thierry Malty
Top right: Indoor pool overlooks the valley through large glass window wall. Photo: Augustin Ochsenreiter
Above: Raw clay covers a heated wall separating bathing and sleeping areas. Photo: Thierry Malty

The Carneros Inn

In picturesque Napa, California, USA, The Carneros Inn is intrinsically related to its surroundings. The Carneros winegrowing district is the southern gateway to the famed Napa Valley, home to ranchers, farmers, and vintners. The Carneros Inn, named after the Spanish word for sheep, evokes Northern California's early-20th-century agricultural and winemaking traditions in its architecture, cuisine, and treatments. Twenty-seven acres (11 hectares) of vineyards overlooking the Mayacamas Mountains are home to the Inn's 86 private guest cottages (each with patio, garden, and outdoor shower), 24 resort homes, the Hilltop gathering space, Boon Fly Café roadhouse restaurant, swimming pool, hot tubs, gardens, and spa.

Outdoor fireplace adds cozy appeal to Hilltop and pool area at The Carneros Inn
Photo: Art Gray

Locally inspired architecture and landscape draw on Northern California traditions. Architect William Rawn Associates of Boston, Massachusetts, USA, creates a stylized barn for Hilltop, whose refined barn-siding and stone work bring added sophistication to the vernacular style. Napa-based interior designer Shopworks uses softly contemporary furnishings in tactile fabrics and rich woods for a home-like feeling. Guest cottages with tin roofs and board-and-batten siding exude country charm, while the interiors are comfortably sophisticated (with heated bathroom floors!). Responsible practices are utilized in the realization of The Carneros Inn, where recycling, geo-thermal heating and cooling, water conservation, and energy-efficient strategies contribute to environmental stewardship.

The unusual treatments at the spa are related to the local environment, falling into categories of Cellars, Minerals, Farms, Creeks, and Harvests. The bounty of the grape is celebrated in Cellars treatments, such as Bulgarian Rose and Grape Seed Facial, which freshens your skin by mixing local grape seeds with imported Bulgarian rose oil (Carneros' owner and spa director are of Bulgarian descent). As you might expect, Minerals includes volcanic stones, seaweed, salt, sugar, and magnesium oxide. Healing Gem and Stone Massage uses solar-charged aromatherapy oils and warm and cold volcanic stones; seven semi-precious gems are placed on your essential chakra points. The natural benefits of goat's milk, mustard seed, maize flowers, and blackcurrants give Farms treatments their power. Soothing Goat Butter Wrap adds elasticity to your skin with aloe vera infused with goat-butter moisturizer. Go to Creeks to bathe in the Huichica Creek Bath, where a steady stream of warm water relaxes your body while you soak in goat's milk, sea salts, aromatherapy oils, or mustard seed. Harvests rely on healing herbs, fruits, and flowers, such as ginger, lemongrass, and honeydew. Orchard Olive Stone and Honeydew Exfoliation smoothes your skin with warm crushed olive stones mixed with native Carneros olive oil. After the scrub, you will luxuriate with a honeydew massage, and raise a toast to a more refreshed and relaxed existence.

Above left: Tactile materials highlight stylish furnishings at Hilltop
Above right: Comfortable, modern furnishings pamper guests in their individual cottages
Photos: Art Gray

Opposite top left: Neighboring horses add a pastoral feeling by the pool. Photo: Art Gray
Opposite top right: Guest suites open up to large patios. Photo: Mark Hundley
Opposite bottom: Stylized barn gives the vernacular style a modern twist. Photo: Mark Hundley

Wellness & Medical Spas: Creating Health
By Roger Gabriel

When we create an environment that is nourishing to all the senses, we allow the body's inner healer to emerge. We all experience the world through one or more of our senses. The food we eat, the movies we watch, the weather, our relationships, all influence us, creating nourishment or disharmony in our lives. Much of the time our senses are assaulted by undesirable things in our surroundings—traffic noise, utility poles, unpleasant aromas, and such. To be healing, a spa needs to have a nourishing environment, through embracing architecture, comfortable furnishings, soft fabrics, soothing colors, pleasing aromas, and melodic sounds. Guests must feel at home. Once a guest feels comfortable with her or his surroundings, the process of healing begins.

A healing center should also open the possibility for people to improve the quality of their lives. People come as our guests, and while they are under our care they should feel pampered. Some people think they can drop their body off for a week and it will be fixed. We need to convey the notion that life is a journey, and that by showing them a few signposts along the way, people can learn to participate in their own well-being.

We are our own pharmacies. In order to uncover this tremendous healing power within, we need to spend time with ourselves. One way to spend time with oneself is through meditation. Meditation takes us to quieter levels of the thinking process, allowing us to contact the field of infinite possibilities in the gaps between our thoughts. With regular practice we bring this experience into our everyday lives, creating the life of our dreams. Using meditation, the mind becomes quiet, which then quiets the body. The less turbulent the body is, the more the self-repair, healing mechanisms are amplified.

When we get in touch with our essential nature we begin to see that present-moment existence—even an entire lifetime—is nothing other than a flicker in eternity, a parenthesis in eternity, a little flash of a firefly in the middle of the night in the context of eternity.

With this knowledge and experience, we begin to recognize mortality as quantified immortality. We begin to see time as quantified eternity. When we see it against the backdrop of who we really are, the anxiety of daily

Spa Fusion. Photo: courtesy Freeline Advertising

Roger Gabriel is program director at the Chopra Center in San Diego, California, USA, where he has assisted Deepak Chopra with numerous seminars and workshops, and trained several hundred instructors in meditation and health creation.

existence disappears. We cease to be troubled or overshadowed by the trivial things of daily existence, the little hassles that create stress in most people. Life becomes joyful, and we realize that the present moment is as it should be, that there is no other way. It is the culmination of all other moments and it is the center point of eternity. We begin to pay attention to what is in every moment. And when we do that, we realize that the presence of God is everywhere. We have only to consciously embrace it with our attention. And that's what creates joyfulness. We have to know the reality and the reality is that we are eternal.

Ajune

A sparkling tile façade greets you on the busy Upper East Side of Manhattan, marking the entry to a New York City, USA, refuge for your skin. Board-certified plastic surgeon Dr. Mauro C. Romita created Ajune as a "center for beauty synergy." Offering both aesthetic and clinical care, the on-site nurse, nutritionist, and dermatologist create aesthetic services in response to stress, environment, and time, as well as therapeutic and restorative skin and body treatments. Romita's technique of reversing the aging process centers around sequential intervention—using less invasive techniques at the early signs of aging for as long as possible, only moving to complex surgical enhancements when absolutely necessary.

Ajune's frosted-glass walls are illuminated from within
Photos: Dan Bibb

Creating the beautiful space for Ajune is New York City-based spa specialist Robert D. Henry Architects. Starting with the concept of a sensuous journey, the architect reflects the spa's philosophy of balance and harmony through the use of sensitive materials, color palette, and lighting strategies. You enter from the street-side retail area, and proceed through a proscenium of mossy-green recycled glass tiles that cast a pearl-like reflection onto the warm wood interior. Custom-crafted cabinet walls comprise the Informational Forest, which displays products and information in the dramatically articulated walls and freestanding storage units. To reach the treatment rooms, you travel through the mysterious Hall of Whispers—an elongated passage with a glowing veil of white scrim, which is infused with the sound of falling water, bringing greater calm and further animating the space. Quiet alcoves with intimate lighting and soft aromatic scents have been created for your privacy and reflection. Each spa room—or Sanctuary—is designed to help facilitate and provide maximum comfort and serenity during care sessions. Candlelighting, hand-rubbed finishes, wafting scents, and calming sounds complete the mood.

Aiming toward total body health, Ajune recommends starting with a Biological Terrain Assessment, a scientific method that evaluates your health. From there, a nutritionist might order the Facial du Jour, which uses fresh fruits, vegetables, grains, and essential oils matched to your specific needs. Personalized treatment is a large part of the synergistic approach at Ajune. Specially designed programs include Wisdom, offering weight-loss through nutrition, yoga, and Eastern bodywork; Purification, body detoxification in a three-day cleansing program with yoga, lymphatic drainage, and hydrotherapy; and Metamorphosis, stressing weight-loss through fitness, nutrition, and endermologie (body contouring) treatments. Prior to having any clinical services, you will undergo a consultation with a registered nurse who might prescribe peels with alpha-hydroxy, salicylic, or fruit acids, or using a controlled stream of natural salt crystals to remove layers of damaged skin. Procedures use pharmaceutical-grade concentrations that are administered only by medical professionals. Once only conducted in hospitals, many procedures are done in on-site surgical suites, defining the medical spa as a beautiful alternative to clinical care.

Above: The Informational Forest greets you on arrival
Left: Ajune's storefront enhances a busy city street

Above: Diaphanous scrims and the sound
of water glide you to the treatment rooms
Right: Treatment sanctuaries are designed
for comfort and beauty

Skinklinic

Long-time skincare and cosmetics executive Katherine Dwyer envisioned a "skincare clinic that feels like a spa." Thus was born Skinklinic, the first one opening on upper Fifth Avenue in New York City, USA (with additional United States sites in Connecticut and Las Vegas). Offering cutting-edge services for both men and women, Skinklinic knows you're busy, so it structures quick, walk-in treatments that promise visible results. Having anything but a medical feeling, the cool contemporary space merges the luxury of a spa with the science of skincare.

Skinklinic's architecture recalls Mies' Barcelona Pavilion
Photos: Dan Bibb

Like skin itself, the spa's design is a network of layers of transparency and translucency. The modern and clean space by New York City-based Richardson Sadeki Design starts to reveal itself behind black slate walls. A dramatic entry path leads you across a reflecting pool—literally transporting you from the grimy city into the clarity of the clinic. The designers looked to influences as direct as Mies van der Rohe's modernist Barcelona Pavilion and as evocative as Claude Monet's Impressionist *Waterlillies*. Once inside, the sparse palette of slate, glass, and wood creates an inviting atmosphere accented by colors of rust orange, cream, and the spa's signature purple. Adding interest to the refined color scheme is a variety of materials—glass-enclosed plastic partitions, synthetic leather and suede on seating elements, rubber and epoxy flooring, and richly grained wood cabinetry.

Before any treatment is given, your skin will be the subject of analysis ("skinscription") so the registered nurses can customize the proper skincare plan. Hydroxy acids—both alpha and beta—are used in treatments that exfoliate skin to increase its performance and allow fresher skin cells to surface. Glycolic treatments use the alpha-hydroxy acids, which are usually derived from fruit and milk sugars, to decrease wrinkles and increase collagen and elastin production. The Beta treatments use salicylic acid to break down whiteheads and blackheads for renewal of oily skin. Lasers are used for collagen stimulation, spot removal, acne treatments, capillary removal, and hair termination. Also featured are microdermabrasion, Botox® injections, and IPL (Intense Pulsed Light) that repairs sun damage and age with high intensity bursts of light. Your skin's many layers may never be the same.

Far left: To meet your busy schedule, walk-in services are performed quickly
Left: Light and color play off reflective surfaces

Above: A path through the water delivers you to Skinklinic
Right: Transparent and translucent surfaces evoke layers
of radiant skin

Chiva-Som International Health Resort

At the beachside location of Chiva-Som, the name's meaning—Haven of Life—is interpreted literally. The wellness spa is unique to Thailand, and sits on the country's eastern seaboard in the royal resort town of Hua Hin. Combing sybaritic pleasures with medical awareness, Chiva-Som is committed to your holistic being. Mind, body, and spirit are equal in all areas, from fitness programs and spa treatments, to medical consultations and healthful cuisine.

Thai pavilions sit within the lush landscape of Chiva-Som International Health Resort
Photos: Pavan Bali

Equilibrium comes into play in the design, as United Kingdom-based architect Syntax Group balances between Thai and Western motifs. You may opt for a guest pavilion in traditional Thai architecture surrounded by tropical gardens, lakes, and waterfalls. Or, Western-style guest rooms offer terraces overlooking the Gulf of Siam. In either case, natural materials, such as wood, marble, and hand-glazed ceramics contribute to your feeling of inner calm and peace. Lobbies and lounges have large windows to bring in natural light and sumptuous views. As a beach resort, water plays a large role, both in therapies and in design. You'll find a beachside pool, indoor pool, waterfalls, marble-and-glass hydrotherapy suite, and plunge pools.

Your options continue as you choose among luxurious spa treatments and medical wellness programs that stress the positive aspects of prevention and well-being. Doctors and nurses, as well as nutrition, exercise, and fitness advisors, will conduct a health consultation to determine treatments and activities for your stay. Most treatments are related to Chinese medicine, yet look to Western practices as well for programs on stress-relief, cardiac rehabilitation, smoking cessation, bolstering the immune system, weight-loss, etc. Some of the unusual programs include: Oxygen Power Fitness, exercise with vitamin, mineral, and oxygen intake; Iridology, analysis of organs and body systems by examining markings in the fiber structure and color of the iris; Equilibropathy, which looks at the spinal column and associated muscles to determine problems then remedies them with acupuncture; and Chi Nei Tsang, an internal organs massage around the navel and abdominal area. Water therapies include a flotation room, where you float in a 10-inch (25-centimeter) saline solution for deep mental relaxation. A more vigorous water treatment is Body Jet Blitz for detoxification, circulation stimulation, and lymphatic flow. You still need some pampering for true, holistic health, and Chiva-Som features heated herbal packs for the Thai Herbal Massage, and the moisturizing properties of fruit, herbs, and flowers in the Papaya Wrap. Your ultimate splurge, however is the Bath of Chiva, where you bask in a candlelit hydrating milk bath sprinkled with rose petals and chamomile flowers. A haven, indeed.

Above: Four outdoor massage areas allow greater connection with nature
Opposite: Thai guestrooms are made from natural materials

Above: The outdoor pool doubles as a site for water sports
Right: You are suspended in 10 inches (25 centimeters) of saline water in the Flotation Tank
Opposite: From the pool, you gaze onto the sea

Blue Medical Beauty Spa

Evoke the color blue, and you bring to mind clarity, sky, water, and, above all, health. These themes are well explored at Blue Medical Beauty Spa, located on the busy main thoroughfare in Sherman Oaks, California, USA, near Los Angeles. The historical La Reina Theater has been transformed into this up-to-the-minute medical spa oasis offering a broad range of treatments. Laser removal of hair, veins, and tattoos (big in the entertainment-industry capital) are offered, along with wrinkle-reducing Botox® injections (also popular in "the industry"). Therapeutic and relaxing massages, as well as a full manicure and pedicure menu, round out the offerings. There's also a juice bar for concoctions to heal you from within.

An historic theater is given new life as Blue Medical Beauty Spa
Photos: Ayola Photography

Blue is a lively antidote to both big-city life and generic design. Los Angeles-based Michael Marquez Architects created a crisp, contemporary, and playful design in the 6,000-square-foot (555-square-meter) space. The building's previous life as a 1950s movie theater is acknowledged with the Blue sign in the marquee and the ticket booth transformed into an information kiosk. Inside, deep sparkling blue tones combine with crisp white for a hip take on a medical look. The feeling is anything but hospital-like, as sinuous curves—recalling the spa's wave logo—weave through the space. Behind the glowing reception desk is a dramatic glass wall with a sandblasted wave pattern and flowing water, while the ceiling is adorned by white and blue cloud-like abstractions. The fabric tensile structures create a fluid ceiling look to mitigate the old theater's high ceilings. Vertical surfaces are tiled with small blue and white mosaics. Walls and partitions sport porthole-like apertures for product display. More swirls envelop you in the embracing modern lounge furniture upholstered with comforting and lush velvet. Hallways are lit from below with blue neon that acts as a glowing guide through the space. The neon and illuminated reception desk are on at all hours, becoming beacons of health projected to the active street beyond. Denim-wearing therapists bring you to treatment rooms, where practically every surface is a shade of blue—from the palest robin's egg to the deepest azure.

Laser treatments are the specialty here, but there is a host of additional non-surgical solutions for your skin's problems. The FotoFacial is a non-laser treatment of photorejuvenation to improve the appearance of the skin through a series of gentle pulses of visible light delivered onto the surface of your skin. Relaxing, hydrating, and therapeutic facials and customized masks also bring your skin to a beautiful state of equilibrium. Reduce your cellulite through mesotherapy, where the middle layer of your skin (the mesoderm) gets microinjections of conventional or homeopathic medication or vitamins. Body contouring occurs with endermologie, which was originally invented to remove scars, but also increases skin circulation using a patented mechanism with unique rollers and a special vacuum. Facial peels, microdermabrasion, and dermaplaning will also leave your skin clear and healthy, and your mood anything but blue.

Above: Saturated blue tones calm you in the treatment rooms
Left: Porthole openings showcase product
Opposite left: Various textures of white—glass, water, plastics, and fabric—play off radiance and transparency of skin
Opposite right: White ceiling fabric is stretched for cloud-like effect

Spa Fusion

Finding spirituality in the urban context is not easy, but Spa Fusion aims to bring your body, spirit, and mind together in the ultra-modern MegaFit health club in Shanghai, China. Located in an active business hub thought of as Shanghai's Times Square, MegaFit's massive glass building is a fishbowl of activity, from socializing in the bars and restaurants to training in the myriad fitness facilities. Aiming to impart experiences that are simple, perfect, and authentic, Spa Fusion considered eight elements in the creation of the spa: water, nourishment, movement, touch, aesthetics, environment, culture, and contribution. All of these fuse to bring you physical and mental enjoyment and transformation.

Hot-stone massage is enjoyed on amorphous wooden decks at Spa Fusion
Photos: courtesy Freeline Advertising (unless noted)

Employing glazed instead of solid walls, Shanghai architect BAU International created a voyeuristic sense to the building. Huge glass window walls afford views of swimming pool and exercise rooms, while letting the landscape and life of the city into the building as well. The tension between open and closed continues in the third-floor spa. Light and transparency from four sides of the building, plus skylights, are moderated by lush silk and satin curtains. The red, saffron, and white materials delineate treatment rooms, and are drawn when rooms are in use. When rooms are free, transparency comes back, and you can gaze from the glass in the reception through the four treatment rooms. Treatment areas are color themed: rain room is gold, cloud room is white, wind room has earth tones, and heaven room is bronze.

Your Spa Fusion experience can include a number of facials for hydration, balancing, and cleansing. Most noted is the Royal Jelly facial, an anti-aging treatment with royal jelly ampoules and mask, combined with collagen massage cream. Give your body the same treatment with Royal Jelly for Body, often followed by a session with a micro-current toning and lifting machine. Oxy-Vita Booster draws on oxygen therapy to increase your energy level, boost your immune system, combat stress and anxiety, calm your nervous system, and kill infections. For complete relaxation, the Crystal Clear Ear Spa clears your ears with ear candles, which are followed by an ear bath and lifting massage for shoulders, neck, face, and scalp. The treatment ends with a cool mask that makes your mind as clear as glass.

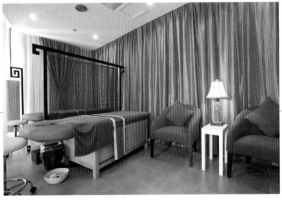

Above: Hydrotherapy is conducted in the white "cloud" room
Opposite top: Glass and colorful drapes set the design tone in the spa's lobby

Opposite left to right:
Glass replaces solid walls for ultimate transparency
Bright satin and silk drapes create privacy in treatment areas
Glass, metal, wood, and water fuse in a modern design. Photo: courtesy BAU International

Day Spas: Seizing the Day By Shenyn Wang

Spas have become essential to modern life. We spa during business trips, on cruise ships, or just to get spoiled during a destination spa getaway. However, most people cannot (spiritually) afford to wait six months to a year to take the spa vacation they sorely need. A day spa visit is the perfect remedy for city dwellers that seek frequent stress relief.

Creating a spa experience in a day-spa environment is not an easy job; it is a special challenge both from a design viewpoint as well as from an operational one. As it is usually situated in the middle of the city, surrounded by all the sources of stress in everyday life, a day spa must have the ability to instantly shield you from the outside world. When we need to quickly recharge in the midst of busy city life, we really don't want a chocolate body wrap or a Balinese flower bath while gazing out of the treatment room window at a view of rush-hour traffic. We want to unload our stress and have radiant skin, or relieve a headache while enjoying a stone massage. The best day spas make people forget where they actually are.

As day-spa patrons have a limited few hours out of their day to relax and rejuvenate, they seek efficient, smooth service in a well-designed space. There is no time for sipping mint welcome drinks with a mini-umbrella while waiting for check-in at a reception sofa. Moreover, as most day spas are located in the city, where space is precious and there isn't the luxury of natural resources, such as a great view or open space to enhance the spa mood, day-spa design must innovatively create a spa atmosphere from scratch. Great day spas reward their customers by garnishing their world with a virtual paradise, such as indoor greenhouses, water elements, breathtaking lighting design, exquisite treatment rooms, luxurious amenities, and relaxing lounges.

Another aspect of day spas that makes them unique among spa formats is that most customers are long-term, repeat customers. They integrate the day spa into their life. The best day spas are multifunctional, with well-organized services: massages focusing on stress relief, facials providing clean and youthful skin, or Vichy showers with body scrubs to slough off fatigue. After all the relaxation and special care, then you can finish with a perfect manicure and a healthy, energetic lunch.

From a spa operator's viewpoint, the frequent visits of day-spa guests means that the relationship between the spa and its customer becomes vital. Spa personnel must have stations that are obscure within the spa environment,

Orient Retreat Spa. Photo: Roy Lee

Shenyn Wang, an active member of International Spa Association (ISPA), is chief operating officer of Orient Retreat, which owns a network of 16 spas and seven retail shops within Taiwan, the United States, and Canada.

yet readily accessible should service be desired. Even the atmosphere must be delicately balanced, as customers cannot become bored—or worse, annoyed—by the decoration after a few visits. Spaces must be designed to be flexible for frequent changes, while still maintaining a high-quality setting. In the end, spa-goers must be more comfortable coming to the day spa than they are going home.

According to the International Spa Association's definition, a day spa is "a spa offering a variety of professionally administered spa services to clients on a day-use basis." In other words, a day spa is a temporary escape from a hectic workday, like an oasis in a city. People living the modern life can't avoid stress, but we can breathe it out regularly at day spas. We relax, recharge, and move on.

Banyan Tree Shanghai

Shanghai, China, has become one of the world's destination cities. However internationally urbane, its Asian traditions are also celebrated at the Banyan Tree Shanghai day spa. Part of the global hospitality company that specializes in remote, luxury locations, Banyan Tree Shanghai brings the feelings of romance, serenity, and exotic sensuality to a city environment. The Asian tenets of feng shui and yin yang inspire the spa's generations-old techniques used to deliver health and beauty remedies to urban sophisticates.

Sumptuous silks and a crackling paint finish create the feeling of Fire in one of the "elemental" treatment rooms at Banyan Tree Shanghai
Photos: courtesy Banyan Tree Hotels & Resorts

The entire experience at Banyan Tree Shanghai is based on the five elements of earth, gold, water, wood, and fire. Treatment rooms reflect each theme through Singapore-based Architrave Design and Planning's detailed appointments. Earth, which symbolizes optimum balance by regulating the elements, is represented by a room of brown tones with walls lined in rough, ashlar masonry. Shimmering with warmth is the Gold room, where gold-leaf walls and auric horns announce its gifts of purification, prosperity, and radiance. Sleek and modern, the Water room is designed for rest, stillness, and meditation. There might be numerous obvious ways to represent Wood, but the element's attributes of new life, growth, and renewal are creatively displayed by thin wooden slats placed over glowing white walls. A crackling paint finish in hot red creates the vitality and energy of the Fire room. Silk-covered treatment tables, coordinating sofas, and an embossed sign representing each element's symbol further adorn the rooms.

The elemental themes are carried into your treatments, which use a wide range of aromatic oils, herbs, spices, and other ingredients with ancient healing properties. Earth treatments promote even distribution of energy through the body with a Lulur Scrub, using the purifying qualities of Indonesian herbs. Bounty from the earth contributes to your Ginseng Nourisher facial mask for intense moisturizing. Purification through the Gold program is achieved with exfoliating Black Sesame Scrub and detoxifying Volcanic Purifier Wrap, as well as the Peaches and Cream facial using pure pearls and peach extracts for a classic complexion. Moisture is returned to you in Water treatments, such as Apple Polisher, which exfoliates and hydrates with fruit enzymes and honey, Rice Pearls Conditioner bolstered by glutinous rice and ginseng, and a cool Honey Cucumber Mask to return balance to your skin. Milk and honey infuse the sumptuous Empress Bath, where you'll be lowered into a rose-petal wonder. Renewal rings true to the Wood services, including relaxing White Lotus Enricher for your body and fruit-infused Tangy Scrub and Cherry Mask for your face. Fire treatments actually cool the heat through Golden Gram Scrub blended with mung beans, Jasmine and Green Tea Conditioner, and Pearl Lustre facial mask. Treatments taken separately or in specific combinations aim to bring your yin and yang into elemental harmony.

Top left: The day spa's lobby seamlessly blends Asian and contemporary thought and design
Bottom left: Brown tones and rough stone define the Earth treatment
Above: In addition to prosperity, Gold's powers include purification

Above: Empress Bath douses you with milk, honey, and rose petals
Top right: Calming colors create a Water space of cool repose
Bottom right: Dark slats are creatively placed atop glowing white walls in the Wood room

Left to right:
Pearl Lustre facial mask cools and calms your skin
Jasmine and Green Tea Conditioner cleanses and moisturizes
Intense moisture is achieved with the Ginseng Nourisher

Green apples and honey are gentle exfoliants used in the Apple Polisher
White Lotus Enricher is applied with delicate strokes to relax your body and mind

E'SPA at Gianfranco Ferré

Milan is Italy's fashion capital, and Gianfranco Ferré is one of Italy's more daring designers. When he wanted to add to his art of decorating the body from without to healing the body from within, he turned to noted spa provider E'SPA for a glittering collaboration. Nestled within the fashion designer's boutique complex, this spa is a sophisticated palace of repose and respite. The quest for balance between the mind and body is the mission in a series of holistic treatments aimed at equilibrium, serenity, rejuvenation, purification, rebalancing, revitalization, and new beginnings (for pre- and post-natal times).

Interior courtyard garden at E'SPA at Gianfranco Ferré removes you from the urban environment
Photos: Paola de Pietri

Milan architect Ezio Riva worked with Ferré to create a place of exquisite beauty and relaxing aura. Like he does with his fashions, Ferré designs to exude sophisticated elegance with a structured, modern flair. Black and brown glass mosaic tiles line the floors that lead you past geometric rose and briarwood reception furniture to a garden relaxation room. Body-contoured loungers face the garden, giving you a surprising, natural escape from the bustling city beyond. Walls of waxed stucco and shiny wood combine with the original stone of the building, bringing home the notion of new and old. Lighting uses chromotherapy, changing color through invisible neon tubes depending on treatments and time of day. Treatment rooms are simple, but no less sumptuous with copper halo ceilings, soft upholstery, and marble basins. Glistening gold glass mosaics shimmer in the mud chamber shower and infusion room.

You will begin your day at Gianfranco Ferré with an enveloping five senses experience: seeing the beautiful design, listening to Tibetan cymbals, inhaling pure aromatic essential oils, drinking herbal infusions, and feeling a footbath and energy-point massage. After that, you are ready for Holistic Total Balance, which entails full-body exfoliation, followed by a deep body, face, and scalp massage with hot and cold stones and a special blend of essential oils. A therapeutic service for cellulite-sensitive areas is the Stimulating Hip and Thigh Treatment, which includes exfoliation with seaweed-salt scrub followed by detoxifying massage and application of warm marine algae; essential reflex points on your feet and eye area are activated to continue the purifying and cleansing process. To show off the latest revealing fashions you'll want a Life-Saving Back Massage with exfoliation for circulation and cell renewal, aromatherapy massage, and warm mud mask. In the Mud Chamber, cover your body and face with a mixture of mud, chalk, and healing earth. After you allow the mud to dry to leach toxins from your system, the chamber fills with herb-infused vapors to soften the mixture, which you then rinse in the sparkling shower with a Midas touch.

Above: Vitality pool is filled with hot mineral water for hydrotherapy
Left: Sparkling gold glass lines the Mud Chamber shower
Opposite top: Mud Chamber fills with herb-infused vapors

Opposite bottom, left to right:
Sleek, modern design welcomes you to the spa
Loungers conform to the body
Candle-like light fixtures add an artistic flair

Orient Retreat Spa

The new flagship location for the growing Asian day spa network of Orient Retreat in the town of Taichung, Taiwan, glows with beauty and radiance. A growing city a couple of hours from Taipei, Taichung boasts a more bucolic environment than its neighboring metropolis. Orient Retreat Spa caters to an upscale clientele of housewives and business executives through its mission as a full, lifestyle spa. Spa education workshops, in addition to pampering and therapeutic treatments, contribute to the lifestyle element. Located in an emerging neighborhood that is gaining momentum as a wellness enclave, Orient Retreat contributes to the community with its public courtyard garden and café, open to spa and non-spa patrons alike.

A lighted, halo-like entry welcomes you to Orient Retreat Spa
Photos: Tim Griffith

You receive a welcoming embrace from New York City, USA-based Robert D. Henry Architects' design. Orient Retreat Spa's corner location addresses the street and connects with passersby. Limestone walls line the street front and give way to the corner entrance, where you glide under a literal circle of light (more figuratively, think: halo) to begin your retreat. As you step up to the open and inviting garden, you experience the senses of sight, taste, smell, and sound as you gaze upon the L-shaped reflecting pool with floating islands that sport an outdoor café as well as aromatic trees surrounded by dancing water that creates natural music. The 7,000-square-foot (650-square-meter) sanctuary inverts the expected—the second floor of local limestone is a heavy mass above the delicate glass of the ground floor. You enter by crossing a wooden bridge over the reflecting pool and into the reception area. By making the entry ceremonious, the architect aids in your physical transformation from the outside world to your inner retreat. Interiors, which were created with the assistance of Taipei-based interior designer Thomas Wang, evoke a clean and clear feeling with the use of local redwood and contemporary furnishings. Changing areas, lounges, café, and tea and juice bar are all oriented toward the garden. An elegantly detailed, light-filled stairway takes you to 15 treatment rooms and the relaxation lounge on the second floor overlooking the garden, where bubbling water sets a meditative tone. The couples' room provides a poetic vignette of nature by focusing on a single tree illuminated by the open light-well above. A magical mood pervades the spa with soft light flowing through diaphanous window treatments and ceiling coves.

In such a setting, relaxation and purification are natural goals. Orient Retreat Spa organizes services in six themes: mind body purification (massage), facial pampering, body treatment, slimming and firming, extreme care (for hands and feet), and the retreat (themed treatments). Body scrubs refresh and exfoliate with salt or yogurt–lavender mixture, while wraps envelop you in moor mud or spicy Balinese Boreh. The intriguing Golden Spoon Facial features herbal skin care for circulation improvement with two pairs of warm, 23-carat-gold spoons working auricular magic. Wet treatments include Vichy Shower with herb powder and yogurt for deep exfoliation, followed by warm water jets raining on your body. Only Aroma Retreats feature facial care and body massages with nature essences of your choice. This ex-urban retreat also offers Busy Bee Facial, Metro Escape, and Quick Relaxation for those on the go.

Left to right:
Café tables sit on a floating island
Natural light bathes spaces through diaphanous drapery
Café and garden courtyard are open to the community

Above: Cross a wooden bridge over the long reflecting pools
Opposite: Indigenous trees and spouting fountains highlight outdoor water feature

Rogner-Bad Blumau

Bad-Blumau, previously better known as an agriculturally dominated Austrian village, is now famous for its spa environment of Rogner-Bad Blumau. Just an hour or two from Vienna or Graz, this 100-acre (40-hectare) wood is a complex of hot pools, medical/therapeutic facilities, outdoor recreation areas, restaurants, bars, hotels, and water park. Capitalizing on natural hot springs from the Vulkania, Melchior, and Balthasar sources, Rogner-Bad Blumau boasts a total water area of 27,000 square feet (2,725 square meters). All this lies among artfully designed buildings and green rolling hills.

The gentle cleansing of hay is performed at Rogner-Bad Blumau
Photos: Hans Wiesenhofer

Part Dr. Seuss, part Antonio Gaudí, with a little bit of both Gustav Klimt and Salvador Dali thrown in, the fanciful buildings and interiors of Rogner-Bad Blumau are from the fertile creative mind of Austrian artist and architect Friedensreich Hundertwasser. An early proponent of ecological standards in architecture, Hundertwasser was nicknamed "architect-healer," a fitting sobriquet for the creator of a place that features therapeutic waters and a range of healthful activities. You will find nary a straight line among the undulating rooflines and mosaic-clad interiors. Indoor and outdoor pools are curvy forms that contrast with the whitewashed walls around them. Nature abounds in many gardens and sodded roofs, where you may set up a lounge chair for sunbathing and relaxing.

You will not lack for activities, as outdoor recreation includes golf, horseback riding, tennis, and hiking through the verdant landscape. For pursuits that are more relaxing, there are several indoor and outdoor thermal and freshwater pools, some with underwater music. You can take your pick from a broad range of sauna experiences: Finnish, Swedish, Turkish, bio-sanarium, herb-sanarium, Turkish steam bath, Roman sweat bath, aroma cave, and sauna grotto. The FindeDich holistic health center offers both Western and Eastern therapies. There are also treatments that call on local customs, such as Austrian blood cleansing, detoxifying wrap with rügen chalk from Northern Germany, and local hay bath, which is lightly stimulating in its use of hay that is gentler on the system than mud and fango. In an artful merging of creativity and caring, the Aphrodite Bath offers you a soak in saffron, honey, and mare's milk in a tub room adorned with lush mosaics and the glow of candlelight.

Top row, left to right:
Fanciful architecture exhibits no straight lines
Outdoor water park is one of the highlights
An organic pattern of windows enlivens the buildings

Bottom row, left to right:
Indoor hot pool meanders through the facility
Colorful tile mosaics recall the work of Gaudí
Natural wood and terra cotta warm the bright colors

Evian Spa by Three

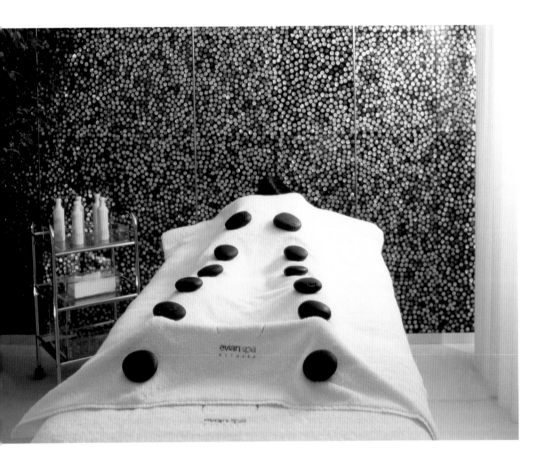

Shanghai, China, is a most cosmopolitan city with a rich history of European influence. So it's no wonder that the first Evian spa outside of France would settle here. In the building Three on the Bund, which sits on Shanghai's historic boulevard along the Huangpu River, French beauty traditions meet Eastern holistic therapies. A women-only facility, Evian Spa by Three has a masculine counterpart, Barbers by Three, a relaxing salon for mens' grooming and neck/shoulder massages. High-end retail boutiques, restaurants, an art gallery, and a music lounge are also at Three on the Bund, which underwent a $50-million restoration by famed American architect Michael Graves.

Mother-of-pearl disks are imbedded in the walls of a treatment room at Evian Spa by Three
Photos: courtesy Three on the Bund

On the second floor, a 115-foot-high (35-meter) atrium entry welcomes you to the serenely beautiful space designed by Hong Kong-based Alan Chan Design Company. Swirling patterns in the carpet imitate radiating rings of water droplets around natural rocks, forming a virtual rock garden. This soothing passageway begins your transition from lively city to inner peace. Lacquered white surfaces and frosted glass form the inner corridors leading to individually designed treatment rooms. Floor troughs of blue neon rim the edges, forming a conceptual stream around the rooms. Slick white gives way to texture and material in each of the themed treatment rooms. Burnished copper paneling lends warmth and emphasizes the element's intrinsic healing properties. Walls imbedded with luminous mother-of-pearl disks reflect your own inner radiance. A natural, earthy tone envelops the bamboo room, while seashells exude the health and freedom of the ocean.

A full slate of treatments allows you to come for manicure and pedicure (including the Luxury Shanghainese Pedicure) or to experience a day of total care and beauty. Coming from France, the Digi-Esthetique facial massage increases circulation and approves the skin's appearance. For total body detoxifying, there's Color Hydrotherapy Underwater Massage or energy-balancing Hawaiian lomi lomi massage. Slimming, contouring, and skin brightening treatments use thalassic ingredients, while the Evian Exfoliating Body Scrub is replete with apricot kernels and marine and herbal extracts for sloughing, along with refreshing bergamot, uplifting jasmine, and toning kaffir lime. With your treatments you'll enjoy relaxing rose tea, made with Evian water, of course.

Top left: Seashells reflect your inner glow
Top right: Burnished copper has healing properties
Above: Hydrotherapy with massage jets and colored light aids circulation

Left: Blue light rims individually designed treatment rooms
Right: A virtual rock garden welcomes you to the lobby

The Greenhouse

There's no busier place than Midtown Manhattan in New York City, USA. On classy 57th Street—home to Tiffany & Company, Bergdorf Goodman, Van Cleef & Arpels, and countless art galleries—is The Greenhouse, a day-spa version of the Dallas institution destination spa. Unlike its female-only Texan counterpart, this Greenhouse offers men and women treatments that combine fine European traditions with ancient Eastern principles and modern technology. The goal, of course, is for you to find serenity, refuge, and well-being.

Step off one of Manhattan's busiest streets into The Greenhouse spa
Photos: Mark Ross

To achieve this lofty goal, New York City-based designer S. Russell Groves creates a serene, three-level spa through consistent use of materials and ingeniously spare construction. Light rift-oak wood covers the custom fixtures and furnishings, which are set upon cork flooring known for its sound-deadening properties. Creamy limestone steps and counters, frosted-glass walls and doors, opaque scrims, and Japanese fabrics contribute to the notion of light, clear materials as your antidote to the barrage of information on the city's streets. Manicure/pedicure stations are made private by high walls that encase television monitors for your entertainment (alternately, you can use a swing-out desk area to catch up on work during your pedicure). Massage rooms, facial treatment areas, and private soaking tubs are all controlled environments focused on your total relaxation. The mezzanine-level café/lounge area is bathed in natural illumination from the skylight—allowing you to ponder the greenhouse theme of renewal.

Your personalized treatments include Signature Facials and Massages tailored to your needs and the Signature Manicure and Pedicure using the lime-ginger Greenhouse Aromatic Scrub to exfoliate skin, lighten dark spots, and even-out color. Medical treatments of Botox®, collagen, chemical peels, microdermabrasion, and leg vein therapies are administered by a dermatologist. Other facials include glycolic treatments, time-erasing lasers, hydrating oxygen, and lightening alpha-hydroxy acids. Healing from the sea is had by an algae body mask and wrap. Men are cared for with the Gentlemen's Facial that includes skin analysis and a custom cleansing and hydrating treatment. For those wishing to totally abandon notions of the city, you can spend One Hour in Tibet. This ayurvedic experience begins with silk-glove exfoliation, continues with warm oil massage, and ends in a purifying rinse that leaves you fresh as budding flora.

Above: Serene, private soaking tub sits in a mosaic-lined room
Top right: Nail treatment stations are made private with tall oak walls
Bottom right: Skylight gives an actual greenhouse effect to the open lounge and café

Left: Treatment rooms are clean and spare for relaxation
Above: Customized water fixture adds drama to the shower/steam room

Destination Spas: Total Spa Immersion by Sonu Shivdasani

With an ever-increasing personal awareness of mind and body wellness, the evolution of the destination spa has been somewhat of an organic progression. This development was a morphing and expansion of the variants rather than a quantum leap. It took the potential of the holistic spa experience to an even higher plateau than that established by many high-end resort spas, creating new opportunities for both the spa-goer and reputable spa operators.

The concept of a destination spa is, in many ways, not new. It was not too long ago that that such establishments may have been referred to as *health farms*, or in a more draconian era, as *sanatoriums*. Europeans traditionally took the *cure,* or took the *waters,* both forerunners of today's model.

Within the destination spa model, there are several sub-models that are best differentiated by the level of mind and body control with which the client feels most comfortable and achieves the most benefit. For some, focused

Six Senses Spa at Madinat Jumeirah. Photo: courtesy Madinat Jumeirah

Sonu Shivdasani is the director of Six Senses Resorts & Spas, focusing on high-end designer resorts and destinations under the brands Soneva Resorts, Evason Hideaways, Evason Resorts, Six Senses Spas, and Six Senses Galleries.

control may be the best environment. For others, a glass of wine with a gourmet meal fulfills the human spirit, and should be enjoyed in order to attain holistic balance.

One significant factor that distinguishes the destination spa is that clients have greater control exercised over them in their treatments and nutritional program, allowing less opportunity to stray from their chosen regimes. In addition to these focused activities, the depth and type of therapies are rapidly expanding. Controlled environments allow more specialization, and—some would argue—provide more positive results when experiencing either traditional or alternative treatments.

A subtle difference between destination spas and resorts spas is that in a resort spa the operator is selling rooms with treatments as an option. The destination spa reverses the dynamics to that of offering treatments as the prime product. The location of a resort will also have an impact on the level of controlled services that can be offered. A resort on a remote island has a better opportunity to offer programs that are similar to that of a destination spa, especially if it also considers the dietary aspects of the program.

The future of destination spas will continue to become more specialized. They will call on experts from other fields to supplement and expand the treatments and therapies offered. Destination and resort spas, however, do have a shared goal of offering the opportunity for personal revitalization through holistic healing and pampering.

The end decision of which model is best suited for an individual is entirely a personal choice. Some of us believe that more control will result in better results; some may see personal freedom from a controlled regime as being the means to ultimate rejuvenation of mind body and spirit.

Red Mountain Resort and Spa

Adventure is certainly in the air at Red Mountain Resort and Spa, so you'll want to be prepared to be active to take advantage of all that is offered here. The majesty of nature will astound you as you gaze at the red and white Navajo sandstone and black lava rock formations in Ivins, Utah, USA. Sitting in the shadow of the 10,000-foot (3,050-meter) Pine Valley Mountain and at the entrance to Snow Canyon State Park, the 55-acre (22-hectare) site is surrounded by Zion, Bryce Canyon, and Grand Canyon National Parks. Rock formations, lava caves, and volcanic cones are there for exploring, while indoor and outdoor pools, tennis courts, and full spa give way to relaxing activities. Red Mountain is in the southwestern part of the state, which enjoys a year-round dry desert climate, making the myriad outdoor activities available whenever you arrive.

Red Mountain Resort and Spa guests explore The Wave, a secret canyon of sandstone domes and carved ravines
Photos: Kim Cornelison

To blend with the stunning natural surroundings, St. George, Utah-based Rich Wells Architects and Scottsdale, Arizona-based interior designer Gaye Ferraras created a series of terra cotta-colored buildings. Nine buildings named after local fauna—such as roadrunner, eagle, big horn sheep—house 116 guest rooms. Buildings are linked by a network of garden pathways abounding with indigenous plants. You can easily navigate among the Fitness Center for health and nutrition classes, Outdoor Recreation Center, and Training Center with workout equipment.

The ethos of Red Mountain is all about health, fitness, and nutrition. An extensive array of outdoor activities includes hiking, kayaking, rock climbing, rafting, mountain biking, rappelling, and more. The core of the program is hiking. Red Mountain's more than 30 trails are offered at various skill levels, along with night hikes to gaze at the moon and stars and learn about astronomy. Education is available in wellness, self-help, relaxation, and all types of fitness—from ai chi to yoga. If that's not enough to do on site, adventure trips to the National Parks and other local sites are available. When you want to relax and pamper your active body and mind, retreat to the spa, where treatments are based on Southwestern and Native American customs. Red Rock Therapy uses canyon stones and juniper oil for deep, relaxing massage. Local ingredients enhance body treatments, such as Mountain Mint Salt Glow with sea salt and fresh mint to uplift your mind and spirit, and Adobe Purification Treatment, which uses rich adobe clay to draw out toxins. Air, earth, water, and fire are represented in the Four Elements treatment, which involves exfoliating native grains, purifying clay, and cleansing and rehydrating juniper oil. Healthy, natural cuisine using organic and free-range products is offered at the Canyon Breeze restaurant, where chefs engage you in cooking and nutrition classes to carry your healthful retreat back into your daily life.

Above: Spa treatments are influenced by Native American customs
Opposite top left: Red Mountain is surrounded by national parks
Opposite top right: Waterfalls, caves, and rocks are there for exploring
Opposite: Bicyclists can navigate through red-rock canyons

Les Sources de Caudalie

In the rolling hills of the legendary French wine country of Bordeaux, a spa exists that takes its mission from its surroundings. Les Sources de Caudalie features Vinothérapie™, which exploits the beneficial properties of vine and grape extracts with natural hot spring water. The discovery that grape-seed extractions combat age-inducing free radicals is the basis of the treatments at the patented Vinothérapie Spa. The spa and hotel are at the property of the Château Smith Haut Lafitte vineyards, an 18th-century country estate with 40 guestrooms and nine suites, outdoor pool, jogging trails, gym, tennis courts, and golf courses, in addition to the acres of working vineyard.

The deep color of Cabernet grapes infuses the water at Les Sources de Caudalie
Photos: courtesy Les Sources de Caudalie

Each room in the Hotel de Charme is sumptuously decorated in tribute to specific people who are passionate about wine—from famous collectors to local folk. Accommodations also include the farmhouse-like Hare's House, situated between the lake and the kitchen garden; an exotic Indian Trading Post with both European and Asian motifs; *Grange au Bateau*, reminiscent of the attributes of water of the Aquitaine region; and the rustic Bird Island house, which is built on stilts within the water for greater communion with nature. The spa building, designed by Paris-based Cabinet Collet-Burger, is a combination of rustic and contemporary feelings. Weathered boards clad the building that has a broad, welcoming lobby and lounge that leads into the indoor Vinothérapie thermal pool. A wood-truss ceiling hangs over the pool pavilion, which is shaded from the open patio by wooden slats, giving you the feeling of bathing within a stylized arbor. Shallow, river-rock-lined moats ring treatment rooms, further emphasizing your connection with nature and the transformations awaiting you.

Grapes and wine form the basis of your treatments, from facials to baths, scrubs, and massages. The Wine Barrel Bath whirlpool places you in a large, round tub reminiscent of an oak wine barrel. Warm spring water enriched with finely crushed grape extracts from seed, skin, stalk, and pulp whirl around you for exfoliation and deep smoothing. Gironde honey is added to wine yeast and organic essential oils for the Honey and Wine Wrap, a hot application that moisturizes your skin and strengthens your immune system. Massages with grape-seed oil and scrubs with grape seeds and honey are available. Some treatments, such as the Pulp Friction Massage, utilize fresh grapes, so are available only during the grape harvest. Also in the harvest season (from September through October) is the detoxifying Grape Cure, a multi-day diet of grapes and red vine herbal tea. (For re-toxing, there's a cigar and brandy lounge!) A varied palate of fresh, seasonal, healthy selections is available—along with a 15,000-bottle wine selection—in the two restaurants located within this intoxicating environment.

Above: The signature Wine Barrel Bath places you in an oaken tub
Right: You traverse rock-lined moats on your way to and from treatments
Opposite top: The spa is surrounded by vineyards and rich mineral waters
Opposite bottom: The continual connection to water is seen in the deck's lily pond

Above: Spa interiors are accented with wood for a feeling of being within the arbors
Right: Jet streams intensify the thermal bath
Opposite top: Off the lounge is the Vinothérapie thermal pool
Opposite left: Only red vine leaf herbal tea is served in the Vinothérapie spa lounge

Six Senses Spa at Madinat Jumeirah

Madinat Jumeirah, The Arabian Resort, has been dubbed City of Senses for good reasons. It's a mini-metropolis of hotels, conference center, health club, water park, dozens of restaurants, souk marketplace, and, of course, the Six Senses Spa, all around 9 miles (15 kilometers) south of Dubai, Saudi Arabia. Alongside a broad stretch of beach on the Arabian Gulf, this resort is a faithful recreation of ancient Arabian architecture, from the meandering waterways and fragrant gardens, to the intricately detailed buildings in various shades of sand color. Next to the famed Burj Al Arab building, a contemporary architectural landmark by UK-based W.S. Atkins and Partners, Madinat Jumeirah is a balanced combination of ancient romance and modern enjoyment.

Semi-tropical gardens surround treatment rooms at Six Senses Spa at Madinat Jumeirah
Photos: courtesy Madinat Jumeirah

The sprawling city was designed by Dubai architects Mirage Mille and includes hundreds of guest rooms in two large boutique-type hotels and a series of 29 courtyard summer houses. Arabian-themed decoration by interior designer Khuan Chew & Associates of Dubai and London features traditional archways, antique-style furnishings, deep wood tones, and sumptuous fabrics. The spa can be reached by foot through the paths in the semi-tropical gardens or by abra, a traditional water taxi. You glide through welcoming wooden doors into more gardens lined with bamboo, palm trees, frangipani, and hibiscus, and into the sensory experience of the spa. Warm earth tones and soft fabrics soothe you in all treatment areas for your journey of spiritual renewal and wellness from within. Lounge areas are infused with fragranced air and the sound of flowing water. Sand-colored granite and stone line the wet-treatment areas that are accented with wooden doors and furnishings. Twenty-six stand-alone treatment studios—each with private garden and balcony—are clustered within a garden courtyard. Outdoor treatment tents decorated with traditional motifs are available for an authentic Arabian experience.

Six Senses bases its treatments on organic ingredients to nourish you both inside and out. Its signature Sensory Spa Journey is an indulgent range of services featuring Four-Hands Aroma massage, luxurious foot bath, and a skin-renewing scrub. A special Crystal Therapy room is used to clear your blocked energy, while Bach Flower Therapy features a system of 38 flower remedies to combat emotional imbalances. To make your face sparkle, the Planet Earth Gem Facial uses oils made with real rubies, sapphires, emeralds, or diamonds, depending on your gem profile. The seductive journey into Velvet Nights begins with a flower-infused bath and ancient body cleansing, continuing with underwater pressure-point massage and incense purification. After you conclude your body exfoliation—with a mixture of nuts, fruits, flowers, and oils—along with an aromatic massage, you will truly know why this special treatment is inspired by ancient stories of love and beauty of Arabia.

Above: Abras water taxis transport you to the spa
Right: Crystal therapy clears blocked energies
Opposite: Couples and friends can share treatment rooms with private terraces

Banyan Tree Seychelles

Serene seclusion awaits you in the Seychelles, a series of 115 islands in the middle of the Indian Ocean. Some are granite islands, some are coral islands. The largest is Mahé Island, home to Banyan Tree Seychelles situated on majestic Intendance Bay. Surrounded by granite islands, Mahé has lush, tropical vegetation on its mountain slopes and a picturesque palm-tree-lined coast. The white beach, azure water, and picture-perfect banana trees prompted 19th-century explorers to assume the Seychelles was the original Garden of Eden. No doubt it was that promise of paradise that prompted actor Peter Sellers and musician George Harrison to own the land that now houses the Banyan Tree.

Dramatic pool melds into the land and sea at Banyan Tree Seychelles
Photos: courtesy Banyan Tree Hotels & Resorts

With the mission to use the sense of place to evoke romance and nostalgia, Banyan Tree's in-house architecture and design firm, Singapore-based Architrave Design and Planning, created 36 private villas that combine contemporary, colonial, and plantation decor, recalling the island's French and British influences. The grand lobby is inspired by plantation homes, while the villas sport broad verandas, louvered doors, and floor-to-ceiling French doors for panoramic views of the bay. You can choose between hillside or beachfront villas, each with private massage pavilions, plunge pools, open-air whirlpools, and high white walls for extra privacy. Rooms are decorated with natural indigenous materials and artifacts to reflect Seychellois culture. Art by local artists is inspired on the island's legendary coco-de-mer coconut.

The spa pampers the human senses and provides a sanctuary of rest, wellness, and pleasure in a distinctly non-clinical approach. Thai, Balinese, and Hawaiian lomi lomi massages are available in your villa or the spa. Scrubs, hair treatments, and body elixirs are crafted from luscious natural ingredients. The Tropical Fruit Scrub swathes you in banana, papaya, watermelon, pineapple, and orange, while the Scented Dill Purifier combines dill seeds with aromatic sandalwood, ground rice grains, honey, and milk. For smooth skin, the Creamy Honey Enhancer envelops you in honey and bananas. Other skin nourishers use green apples, kaffir lime, herbs, and green tea. From the bottom of your toes—with foot baths and scrubs of kaffir lime—to the top of your head—cucumber, rosemary, mint, papaya, sage, and soy hair treatments—your body and soul are smoothed, comforted, and renewed.

Above left: Specially trained therapists perform a range of Asian massages
Above right: Private spa pavilion overlooks the bay

Opposite top: Colonial architecture reflects the island's history
Opposite bottom: Hillside villas afford stunning views of the Bay
Opposite right: The arc of Intendance Bay assures privacy

Mii amo

Set in a private area of the 70-acre (28-hectare) Enchantment Resort, in Sedona, Arizona, USA, is the magical Mii amo spa. *Mii amo* means "journey" in the Native American Yuman dialect, and this spa promises you a journey of self discovery. The Native-American-inspired spa is within Boynton Canyon, a sacred place of Apache myth. Forests and ancient Native American cliff dwelling ruins surround the narrow box canyon, which many believe holds healing powers in its 400-foot-high (120-meter) red rock cliffs. Nestled into the slope of the canyon wall are six casitas with 16 guest rooms, which are designed around interlocking courtyards in a grove of existing cottonwood trees. Made of adobe brick, wood, and indigenous stone, they offer you either a private courtyard or patio. Mii amo guests are welcome to use the facilities at Enchantment Resort, or enjoy the indoor and outdoor pools, library, retail area, fitness center, yoga lawn, juice bar, and café with an exhibition kitchen at Mii amo itself.

Mii amo is nestled in the sacred Boynton Canyon
Photos: Harry Zernicke (unless noted)

The rustic canyon surroundings merge with contemporary architecture by New York City-based Gluckman Mayner Architects. Modern design meets the local vernacular in the 24,000-square-foot (2,230-square-meter) spa. The interior courtyard entrance brings daylight into the building, beginning one of the major themes—light and water—used in the design. As you glide down the grand hallway—a 170-foot-long (50-meter) horizontal circulation spine—you are bathed by sunlight from the continuous skylight on one side. On the other side, five adobe brick towers that recall ancient architectural sites of the Southwest house the treatment rooms. Throughout, simple, meditative spaces are accented by floor-to-ceiling windows offering views of the canyon. The water theme arises in a small stream that originates inside the building and waters a garden of native trees and plants. Water also surrounds the Crystal Grotto—the symbolic heart of the building—created with SPAdesign of Sedona. You step through a covered wooden bridge over a pebble-lined pool into this meditation space. The Grotto connects you to the earth and sky with its oculus at the sun and earthen floor. At the center of the room, colored crystals are embedded in a mineralized trunk of an Arizona ponderosa pine with water flowing within and around it.

Sedona is widely regarded as the headquarters for New Age living, and the treatments at Mii amo follow suit. There are also plenty of modalities using Native American techniques that reflect the healing culture of the Southwest. Mind-body therapies feature crystals, psychic readings, and Human Design, based on astrology, I-Ching, and Kabbalah. A Crystal Bath surrounds you with colorful crystals, essential oils, and soothing sounds. The signature Mii amo Spirit Journey begins with a sage clearing and a chance to state your goals—peace, health, love—before your chakras are anointed with oils. Body Feng Shui begins with a psychic reading and includes an energy-balancing massage. Treatments that are a bit more earthbound are available, such as Sedona Clay Wrap, Blue Corn Vichy, and Soothing Stones Massage. Exercise classes and cooking and health lectures are also offered to complete the journey to your soul.

Left: Petrified Ponderosa pine holds crystals as healing waters flow. Photo: Eika Aoshin

Above: Indigenous colors and materials merge with a contemporary sensibility
Opposite top: Indoor pool is found off the grand hallway
Opposite middle: The grand hallway is flooded with natural light
Opposite bottom: Crystal Grotto encourages meditation and introspection

Daintree Eco Lodge and Spa

Wawu-karrba is the Aboriginal name for this rainforest—meaning "healing of the spirit"—located 90 minutes from Australia's Cairns Airport in Far North Queensland. In this 110-million-year-old site lies Daintree Eco Lodge and Spa, home to the spiritual ancestors of the Aboriginal KuKu Yalanji tribe. Harnessing the potent natural forces of the rainforest to create a healing environment, Daintree blends the local indigenous culture and natural ingredients to offer a back-to-nature spa experience. Morning bird watching (135 recorded species) is a ritual in the 30 acres (12 hectares) of rare land that is surrounded by a World Heritage-listed National Park. Cruises down the majestic Daintree River are enhanced by the year-round average temperature of 80 °F (27 °C).

Rain showers douse you with local spring water from Daintree Eco Lodge and Spa
Photo: Michael Omm

Tropical palms and lush rainforest foliage surround you at Daintree, which infuses nature into your every experience. You can enjoy an Aboriginal interpretive rainforest walk enhanced by natural soft-filtered daylight, oxygen-rich air, and the sound of running pristine rainforest streams and waterfalls. Navigate the property by traipsing elevated boardwalks that meander from building to building. Fifteen individual villas outfitted by Daintree owners Terry and Cathy Maloney—five with balcony whirlpool baths—are set on stilts, with entry available from ground-level or elevated walkways. The innovative cuisine features tastes of cosmopolitan Australian fare with exotic and native ingredients. The covered swimming pool is solar heated, reflecting the spa's environmental ethos.

Aboriginals' local knowledge and techniques are incorporated into treatments using medicinal plants from the Daintree Rainforest, velvety soft ochres from the stream, and pristine water from the property's waterfall. Massage techniques are a combination of aromatherapy and herbalist principles, using an infusion of naturally occurring rainforest flora, wild gingers, and fine clays. The signature Walbul-Walbul Butterfly treatment brings you out of your cocoon by drizzling warm oil on your body and then sprinkling you with desert salt, followed by full-body exfoliation, warm mud wrap, Aboriginal head treatment, rain shower, and relaxing massage. Your tropical experience includes soothing concoctions, such as vanilla-honey body butter, avocado-clay facemask, coffee-wild ginger scrub, coconut-frangipani hair mask, and cucumber-melon shower mousse. As you lay on a hand-crafted timber leaf and are doused with warm showers, your Yiri Julaymba experience mimics what has occurred in the rainforest for eons.

Left to right:
Elevated rooms give you an authentic forest experience
The rainforest spa is infused with the healing spirit
Natural ingredients from the rainforest enhance treatments

A local waterfall feeds hydrotherapy baths
Timber structures are nestled within broad, lush foliage
Photos: courtesy Daintree Eco Lodge

Plateau at Grand Hyatt Hong Kong

Plateau is more than a hotel spa, it's a destination spa that happens to be on the 11th floor of Hong Kong's Grand Hyatt hotel. The 80,000-square-foot (7,430-square-meter) facility includes 14 guest rooms and suites, five fitness and exercise studios, and nine treatment rooms offering relaxation, aesthetics, fitness, and culinary programs. Perched on a landscaped terrace (the high, open flat area defining *plateau*), the spa's outdoor area enchants with waterfall, turtle pond, jogging track, swimming pool, and two restaurants within contemporary gardens that sport more than 1,000 trees. Conceived as a relaxing refuge from the bustling city, Plateau's courtyard overlooks Victoria Harbour. Hong Kong potter Emma Chan was commissioned to create ceramic fish, frogs, and turtles, which can be found throughout the gardens and guest rooms. Other artistic endeavors include dreamy, large-scale black-and-white images of parks, lakes, and gardens by French photographer Vera Mercer.

Plateau at Grand Hyatt Hong Kong's terrace rooms overlook Victoria Harbour
Photos: Vera Mercer

Hong Kong-based architect Morford & Company's design is sleek and calming, affording an indoor/outdoor atmosphere. Dark granite runs through the courtyard, creating water features, tables, and planters for some of the palm and rose-apple trees. Guest rooms overlooking the Harbour or courtyard gardens are decked with wooden platforms, custom futon beds, floor-to-ceiling wood shutters, and oversized bathrooms with private soaking tubs. Geometric blond-wood forms create futon bases, shelves, and cabinetry, all with minimal hardware for a seamless look. Low table and chairs for in-room dining maintain the Asian aesthetic. Two tones of polished granite add accents, but keep the design minimal. Some rooms are equipped with whirlpools and steam baths, while terrace rooms are adorned by bronze falcons gazing at the Harbour.

Mixing elements of European and Asian rituals, spa treatments may be experienced in your room or in specific treatment areas. The Plateau Massage combines shiatsu, Thai, and Swedish techniques, and uses essential oils of your choice for the effect of relaxation (sandalwood, lavender, myrrh), flow (angelica, lemon, cypress), detoxifying (lemongrass, rosemary, geranium), or tonic (rosewood, mint). To exfoliate and soften your skin, Plateau Scrub of raw sugar and green tea is followed by time in the hammam steam room and a toning body balm massage. Body envelopments encase you in clay, sugar, and papaya to relax, or in seaweed and marine-plant extracts to detoxify. A Salt and Pepper Scrub both exfoliates and energizes you for a perfectly seasoned experience.

Left to right:
Ladies' sauna is a great escape from the city below
Low tables and hand-made futons are created for your relaxation
Treatment areas are outfitted with crisp, white furnishings

Above: Turtle ponds and waterfalls add serenity to the dark-granite outdoor space
Right: A granite waterfall anchors one end of the large pool

A jogging path winds through the landscaped terrace

Rajvilas

Sprawling in pure majesty throughout 32 landscaped acres (23 hectares), Rajvilas recalls a bygone era of Indian splendor. Located in the Rajasthani countryside of Northwest India, near Jaipur, Rajvilas is abundant with pools, fountains, and gardens. Purple jacaranda, orange and yellow gulmohar, and red bottlebrush trees create colorful harmony with the pink plaster buildings reminiscent of a traditional Rajasthani fort (albeit one with tennis courts, pools, and putting green). Guest rooms are situated around courtyards, while private villas have their own pools. Fourteen luxury tents offer accommodations that are beautiful and unusual. An 18th-century Shiva temple on a small island in the lotus pond gives even more credence to this spa that specializes in ritual purification from Indian traditions.

Rajvilas is built to resemble a traditional Rajasthani fort
Photos: courtesy Oberoi Hotels & Resorts

Carved elephants guard the entrance of this detailed Rajasthani wonderland by architect P.G. Patki and Associates of Mumbai, India. Traditional building methods and materials play a large part in both the architecture and the interior design by Singapore-based H.M. Lim & Associates. Special touches include hand-painted murals of flowers and birds, lushly embroidered fabrics, Jaipur blue pottery tiles, and traditional Araish wall treatments, which use a mixture of lime and eggshell on the plaster to look like marble. Guest rooms are outfitted with teak four-poster beds and sunken white Italian marble bathrooms overlooking private walled ornamental gardens. A restored haveli, or mansion, houses the 7,000-square-foot (650-square-meter) spa with therapy rooms, suites, sauna, steam rooms, and plunge pools. An outdoor white marble whirlpool awaits you in the courtyard surrounded by a fragrant herb garden.

The spa takes its cures from both Western and ayurvedic treatments. Ayurvedic massage and facials, and shirodhara (pouring of a fine stream of oil on the forehead's "third eye") are available to you, along with a host of treatments using local ingredients. Ayurvedic Marma Point Facial stimulates the marma—vital energy points on the head, face, and ears—with aromatic oils and herbs to both calm and refresh. Based on a royal recipe, the Milk and Rose Bath pampers you with skin-softening milk and skin-toning rose water; a sprinkle of fresh rose petals enhances the regal feeling. Sand Bundle Massage is a mixture of moist and dry applications. After being massaged with aromatic oils, you are gently pounded with small linen bags filled with sand to relieve stiff or swollen joints. Borrowing from India's spice trade is the Turmeric Skin Purifier, a wrap using an age-old recipe with turmeric and sandalwood to refine, heal, and purify you. After the wrap, a guava-yogurt mixture is applied to restore the natural glow of healthy skin. Culinary delights await for dining at Rajvilas, which serves a combination of international and Indian cuisine. Nightly Rajasthani music and dancers in the open courtyard dining area command your other senses.

Above: Courtyards, pools, and gardens grace 32 acres (23 hectares) near Jaipur
Right: Fresh flowers add color and essences to foot treatments
Opposite left: Traditional murals and metalwork are featured in the design
Opposite right: Milk and Rose Bath is derived from a royal recipe

Sanctuary Spa on Camelback Mountain

Situated in the aptly named Paradise Valley, Arizona, USA, Sanctuary Spa on Camelback Mountain is just that: a meditative preserve of 53 acres (21 hectares) high above the valley. Sanctuary's colorful history began in the early 1950s when a group of Hollywood investors bought the property to build an exclusive racquet club. Through a late-1960s movement, the land became a preserve, which halted development above the 1,700-foot (518-meter) level of Camelback Mountain. Terraced into the north slope are 74 mountain casitas, while 24 spa casitas surround the pool and the Sanctuary Spa.

Sanctuary Spa is in the beautiful shadow of Camelback Mountain
Photos: Tom Hopkins (unless noted)

Scottsdale, Arizona-based Allen + Philp Architects and Testani Design Troupe drew from desert design traditions to create Sanctuary Spa. A variety of smooth-trowel stucco geometric forms in desert hues of burnt orange and deep purple comprise the building blocks of the spa. Large-scale masonry paired with floor-to-ceiling glass add elements of earth and light to the indoor/outdoor interplay between public and private spaces. Spa casitas arranged around the meditation garden and reflecting pool are furnished with contemporary pieces mirroring the desert colors. Some of the casitas have their own outdoor steeping tub. Desert sun is kept at bay by billowing fabrics protectively covering the 25-yard (23-meter) lap pool and outdoor rooms. Treatment areas include watsu immersion pool, vitality pool, shower deluge, and the Sanctum, a private outdoor treatment suite for two.

Leaving no mountain stone unturned, Sanctuary Spa offers a range of consultations to impart mental, physical, and spiritual knowledge. Tarot, astrology, inner harmony stress management, QXCI computerized bio-energetic biofeedback system, nutrition, and numerology consultations will give you tools to further your well-being on your own. If equine company is more to your liking, Horse-to-Heart helps connect you with your inner motivations through grooming, walking, and working the horse under the guidance of a certified life coach. For purely sybaritic pleasures, you'll find Ume Plum Roll that revitalizes your body with moisturizing plum and willow extracts. Sumatra Coconut Polish exfoliates with fresh coconut blended with sandalwood, jasmine, vetiver, and clove. Hydra System Facial uses shiatsu, lomi lomi, and lymph drainage to bring radiance to your skin. Taking advantage of the long, warm desert nights, Sanctuary After Dark programs are offered during winter months. Winter Candlelight Watsu is extra magical, as you float in a body-temperature pool lined with votive candles. Stargazing and astrology sessions take place under the night sky, while Evening Guided Meditation occurs in your private casita sanctuary.

Left to right:
Lap pool is protected by billowing fabrics
Some spa casitas have private steeping tubs
Spa rooms ring a reflecting pool

Desert colors and foliage create a calming mood
Indoor/outdoor treatment rooms face the meditative garden

Top: Geometric forms contrast to the natural landscape
Middle: Contemporary furniture in natural materials
highlights spa casitas. Photo: Jim Christy
Bottom: Moonlight programs are offered during winter months

Thalasso Spas: The Ocean Within by Dan Fryda

I still recall my first ocean voyage; it was to France in 1954. Standing along the rail of the RMS Queen Mary, I stared at the endless horizon of blue. The sea mist filled my nostrils with the smell of pure ocean air. A sense of euphoria came over me as I watched the misty salt air cover my navy-blue blazer with white dew. I did not know that by breathing in the sea air, full of minerals and oxygen, I was taking in a revitalizing tonic. Nor did I know that one day I would devote my life to the study and promotion of ocean-based therapies we call thalassotherapy.

The ocean is by far the most abundant mineral-water source we have on the planet. Covering more than 70 percent of the earth, the sea has drawn adventure seekers, poets, and painters alike to contemplate its powerful presence. Its vastness, depth, and beauty never cease to fascinate us.

The lure of the ocean drew the interest of a scientist who discovered our special relationship with seawater. René Quinton was a brilliant French biologist who wrote extensively on the therapeutic virtues of seawater.

In 1904 he published a book entitled *Seawater: Organic Milieu*, which scientifically established the relationship between seawater and human blood plasma. Surprisingly, the water contained in the human blood plasma, which nourishes and flows through our entire being, is chemically and qualitatively identical to seawater. Quinton used this congruency to support his hypothesis that it was from the maritime environment that the first cell came to life. Are we drawn to the ocean because it is, in a sense, the womb of life itself?

So simple, yet so vital, seawater has therapeutic properties. There are so many ways we benefit from the ocean. We bathe in its waters to stimulate circulation. We apply marine seaweed poultices concentrated in potassium, magnesium, and vital trace elements to nourish our skin cells and restore balance. We drink isotonic seawater to detoxify the gastro-intestinal tract, and eat seaweed to chelate harmful radio-active pollutants out of our bodies. We breathe the pure oxygenated sea air to purify our lungs. Seawater, as an

Delos Spa Center. Photo: Dimitris Poupalos

Dan Fryda is founder of Spa Technologies International, which focuses on the development of spa and marine-based products, and a founding member of the International Spa Association (ISPA).

efficient conductor of heat and cold, benefits us when applied to the body by moving blood and irrigating tissues with fresh plasma and oxygen, stimulating lymph drainage, and evacuating toxins that attack our very DNA. Seawater is also a mineral storehouse capable of replenishing vital nutrients. We cannot ignore the power of the sea, for as the eminent Nobel Prize winner Linus Pauling put it, "every disease, every illness can be traced to a mineral deficiency."

All of these unique qualities make thalassotherapy the ultimate balancing experience. It reconnects us to the source of life and helps us cope with and combat the challenges of our modern, stressful way of living. It's the ultimate anti-aging regimen, provided by nature.

Our relationship to the sea and the acceptance of the curative and therapeutic qualities of thalassotherapy has resulted in some 50 destination resort spas known as thalassotherapy stations (the name given to the seawater spas by Dr. de la Bonnadiere in 1869). These spas emerged along picturesque coastlines, especially in France, where 500,000 curists (the name the French gave for those undergoing a week's spa regime) travel each year to experience rejuvenating and revitalizing therapies of the sea. More than half of thalasso centers are in France, but the treatments are gaining popularity around the world, as evidenced by the growing number of spas in Europe, the Middle East, and Mexico.

In thalassotherapy, we like to think that it is the intrinsic relationship of our bodies, the ocean, and life itself that draws us to the treatments of the sea. By embracing the organic identity between the ocean and our bodies we revitalize and energize ourselves. As Quinton pointed out, each one of us is a "walking aquarium filled with seawater." In essence, we go to the ocean that surrounds us to replenish and restore the ocean within us.

Delos Spa Center

What else would bring you back to your inner God or Goddess, but a Grecian retreat? On a hill facing the Aegean Sea, on the beach of Ayios Yiannis, Greece, opposite the sacred island of Delos—reported birthplace of Apollo and Artemis—sits the Delos Spa Center at Mykonos Grand Hotel and Resort. Within Mykonian-style whitewashed buildings adorned with marble mosaics are 107 rooms and suites with private balconies to view the azure Aegean Sea. The landscaped hill steps down to a private beach equipped with chairs and umbrellas. Seawater is enjoyed in the large thalasso pool, and at the ancient beach itself.

Whitewashed forms of Mykonian architecture combine with rustic stone at Delos Spa Center
Photos: Dimitris Poupalos

Bold forms of Greek architecture are mixed with rustic stone in the design by local architect Papagiannis & Associates. The cool whitewash covers the sensual shapes of the buildings, which you navigate through a series of pathways and terraces lined with Doric columns. An amphitheater is set within the rocky hill. Hand-carved marble details recall a glamorous Delian civilization. The Mykonian motifs continue inside, with large archways leading into the guest rooms, each with private balcony or terrace. Interior designer MKV Design of London, England, equipped some rooms with spa-like baths; suites offer swimming pools and traditional Greek barbecues.

As you enter the Delos Spa Center, you'll notice a more subtle version of the familiar design elements—archways, wood accents, and tone-on-tone mosaics. Treatment rooms are named after Greek gods related to beauty: Apollo, Aphrodite, Narcissus, Helios, Adonis. Therapeutic treatments are designed to soothe, pamper, de-stress, and reinvigorate your beautiful god within. Delos prides itself in using all-natural treatments from ancient health and beauty traditions of Greece, such as the signature Nourishing Yogurt, Honey, and Sugar Treatment, which wraps your body in its sweet ingredients. Other body treatments utilize salt, moor mud, and more yogurt, while hydrotherapies douse you with seawater, oils, salts, algae, rose petals, and coconut. You may even indulge in a Glorious Signature Seafront Massage conducted just 35 feet (10 meters) from the water amid the relaxing sound of waves lapping upon the mythic Aegean Sea.

Left to right:
The resort steps down to a private beach
The traditional wooden pergola near the pool houses Aqua e Sole restaurant
Glorious Signature Seafront Massage is done with views of the Aegean

Above: Hydrotherapies bathe you in seawater and healing salts
Opposite: Rest areas are situated outside treatment rooms

Zara Spa

Legend has it that Roman nobles, Cleopatra and Mark Anthony, and the Queen of Sheba looked to the Dead Sea as a source of beauty and luxury. You will, too, at Zara Spa at the Mövenpick Resort on the Dead Sea in Amman, Jordan. Most Dead Sea spas concentrate on the medical benefits of the ultra-dense mineral content of the seawater. Zara, however, is purposely oriented toward luxury relaxation, while still taking advantage of the soothing properties of sea products. Tucked on the northern shores of the Dead Sea, the 64,600-square-foot (6,000-square-meter) resort lies 1,300 feet (400 meters) below sea level. This lowest point on earth enjoys year-round sunshine, dry air, and high oxygen pressure. The sprawling complex includes 340 guest rooms, several restaurants, sports facilities, hydropool, Kneipp foot massage pool, indoor Dead Sea pool, and Dead Sea whirlpool. Of course, you can experience the sea itself, thanks to the resort's private beach.

Hydropool at Zara Spa features neck massage jets and whirlpools
Photos: Jan Kassay

Created as a quintessential Arabian village, the resort is designed by the London office of noted hospitality architects Wimberly Allison Tong & Goo, with Jordanian architect and artist Ammar Khammash, who also oversaw the interiors. The low-profile, two-story village complex is made of indigenous stone dug from the site. Traditional construction methods enhance the authentic feeling of buildings situated around courtyards sprouting olive trees from Bethlehem. Lush gardens surround the bungalows, and a river trickles through the complex. Reminiscent of historical luxury, the spa design is inspired by Jordan's Castle Amra, which served, appropriately, as a bathhouse and relaxation venue during the Umayad Empire (661–750 AD). Inside, the hotel and spa's décor is inspired by Islamic art and architecture. Colorful mosaics in animal and wave motifs also give way to vistas of natural stone that create clear spaces to maintain a sense of tranquillity.

Traditional mosaic patterns also adorn the Turkish hammams in the spa, which feature caldarium, laconium, and rain showers. Healing powers of the sea abound in the various water areas in addition to mud and salt treatments. When you are immersed in the outdoor hydropool, neck massage jets spray heated, lightly salted (3-percent) water to relax you. For higher salt concentration, try the Kneipp foot massage pool and the indoor Dead Sea pool, both with 23-percent salt content. In this mineral-rich water, you'll find calcium to clarify skin, sodium to balance pH, magnesium to enhance skin metabolism, and bromine to relax your muscles. Water also relaxes you with the force of jets for water and shower massages. Instead of total immersion, try dry flotation, where you lie on a warm water bed and enjoy facial massages and mud wraps. Mud therapy encases you in the dramatic Dead Sea black mud, which improves skin texture because of silicates that tighten skin, natural tar that exfoliates, magnesium that hydrates, and clay that moisturizes. Marine algae and plant extracts are used in body slimming treatments and facials that will leave your skin glowing like a legendary beauty.

Top left: The flowers of Jordan surround pools of salt and fresh water

Top right: Dead Sea pool maintains mineral content for soaking

Above: The spa is modeled after an historic castle

Opposite: Courtyards connect buildings, as in traditional Arab villages

Thalassa Spa

Derived from the Greek word for "queen," Anassa has the perfect place for your royal treatment at its Thalassa Spa. Set on the northwest coast of Cyprus' Akamas Peninsula, in the town of Polis, the Anassa resort sits between Latchi Harbor and the Baths of Aphrodite. The hotel, with 184 rooms and suites, features private balconies with louvered shutters in all accommodations for gazing out to the Mediterranean Sea, reminding you of the healing sources of the spa's treatments. The sandy beachfront offers relaxation and water sports. Additional water experiences await you in the mosaic-lined plunge pool, indoor Roman pool, and two multi-level freshwater swimming pools with waterfalls.

Private pools add luxury to suites at Thalassa Spa
Photos: Henri Del Olmo

Conceived by San Francisco, California, USA-based architect Sandy & Babcock International as a Greek-Cypriot village, Anassa comprises several groups of low-rise buildings to blend in with the coastal setting. These structures, with whitewashed walls and low-pitched tile roofs, give you the authentic feeling of inhabiting a Mediterranean hill town. Among landscaped gardens, the "town" also features a church, an organic farm supplying Anassa's restaurants, and the town square. Interiors by James Northcutt Associates of Los Angeles, California, feature Greek motifs, Roman mosaics, and Venetian frescos, all of which pay tribute to the island's former occupants. Rooms are set within gardens and decorated in shades that recall the ocean—coral, aquamarine, green, and white.

Thalassotherapy is the focus here, where seawater is freshly pumped from the Mediterranean and heated to 93 °F (34 °C). The 7,000-square-foot (650-square-meter) spa brings the ocean to you through marine hydrotherapy, algae and mud treatments, saunas, steam baths, and a warm exercise pool with water jets. Body wraps are a soothing way to enjoy the riches of the sea. A detoxifying Sea of Senses Body Wrap uses warmed algae, which is rich in minerals and enzymes. Tension is soothed with marine mud in the Essence of Earth Body Wrap, while legs and hands are relieved of stress with applications of brown seaweed extracts. In the warm algae-infused hydrobath, you are welcome to soak on your own, or enjoy underwater massage both by hand and by powerful water jets. Then relax at the indoor Roman pool, and reflect on your royal treatment.

Left to right:
Anassa is mapped out to resemble a Mediterranean village
Multi-level pools feature waterfalls
The site faces the beach, where water sports are plentiful

Above: Elegant indoor Roman pool is the perfect spot for relaxation
Right: White and stone walls combine with traditional mosaic at the outdoor plunge pool

Left: Warm hydrobath includes water jets for massage
Right: Whitewashed walls and tiled roofs are vernacular touches in the architecture

Miramar Crouesty

All things seaworthy is the theme of the Miramar Crouesty, the hotel and spa shaped to resemble an elegant ocean liner in Arzon, in the seas of Brittany, France. The secrets of thalassotherapy were developed on French shores, from the northern coasts of Normandy and Brittany to the sunny littoral of Biarritz and the Riviera. The long, low building that houses Miramar Crouesty possesses the stately look of a luxury liner that happens to have found anchor in Port Crouesty. The 120 guest rooms and suites—or state rooms, if you will—are outfitted in contemporary styling with ocean touches in nautical blue and white. Architect Pierre Diener opened the rooms to balcony terraces, where you'll enjoy sea views, or feel the refreshing water in the heated seawater swimming pool under a glass canopy. On the top "deck" are both gourmet and low-calorie dining choices, along with a piano lounge for evening relaxation.

Miramar Crouesty resembles an ocean liner going through the seas of Brittany
Photos: Jacques Boulay

A 26,900-square-foot (2,500-square-meter) Louison Bobet seawater therapy institute focuses on fitness and health. Medically controlled programs are administered by doctors and specialists in marine hydrotherapy, algotherapy, and kinesitherapy. Unique to Miramar Crouesty is Aromathalassotherapy, combining seawater therapies with essential oils. Changing with the season, the oils infuse the air in the spa's reception areas, starting your healing upon arrival. Various oils are mixed with seaweed and mud for treatments targeting pain release (pine, rosemary), inflammation (basil, lavender), or slimming (sweet orange, citronella). Aromatic seawater baths will calm you with tangerine and rosewood or stimulate your circulation with peppermint and cypress. For respiration, eucalyptus oil mixes with a fine steamy mist of warm seawater during the Four-Handed Shower. A popular treatment is Manual Affusion—a massage under the constant rain of seawater.

To totally immerse yourself in sea healing, try the Mi Hai, a days-long treatment routine developed and conducted by a Chinese acupuncturist. The series of massages, packs, baths, and Asian modalities aims to balance your energy and guard against external aggressions. You do this by working on the three levels of earth, man, and heavens. Earth is represented by preventative therapies that concentrate on energy by using marine mud and seaweed. Man's level is the balance of circulation through acupuncture and traditional Chinese massage. You reach Heaven when you absorb the energy through breathing by performing Chinese exercises. Intense though it may be, this course—like Miramar Crouesty itself—is a promise of serenity through the sea.

Top: All 120 "staterooms" have ocean views
Far left: Thalasso water course massages you with jets and geysers
Left: Grapefruit adds healing properties to the seawater

Hotel Spas: Check Into Pampering By Michael Adams

Pity the poor traveler a mere decade ago. Weary, out of sorts, sore of muscle and mind. A trip to the average hotel in the average business destination usually meant no more solace for the body and spirit than a desultory visit to a (probably) grungy gym in a (probably) remote corner of the hotel. Maybe there was a pool, but not often an inviting option. It was not much of a reward for the hard-working stiff looking to shed the tension and grime of an attenuated journey.

How things have changed. In an increasing number of hotels, bare-bones gyms and grimy pools have given way to spacious, pristine, and—best of all—sumptuously beautiful spas, whose design is as carefully and imaginatively created as any aspect of the hotel. Perhaps more so.

As one marker of the breadth of this phenomenon, the International Spa Association reports that hotel and resort spas represent the fastest-growing segment in the spa industry, from 473 hotel spas in the year 2000 to 1,662 in 2004. That translates into revenues for hotel companies that approach $5 billion a year.

No wonder hotel companies are so warmly embracing the trend. Take the Four Seasons, which has set the standard for customer service. The company's spas, both hotel and destination, continue the legacy of personal pampering for each guest. Even global chains are getting creative. Hyatt has been adding spa floors among some of its upper-echelon properties, where guests needn't even leave their rooms to enjoy certain spa amenities.

The Spa at Mandarin Oriental, New York. Photo: George Apostolidis

Michael Adams is editor in chief of *Hospitality Design*, the leading trade magazine on hotels, restaurants, spas, leisure facilities, and senior living, and is a frequent participant in hospitality and spa conference programs.

That hotels are pulling out all stops to treat guests with maximum care should come as no surprise to anyone who has paid attention to the industry of late. Competition is fierce, and, especially since September 11th, travelers want to be cosseted, pampered, and made to feel more secure than ever. After conquering the bed, the industry took aim at the bathroom, creating environments much more spa-like and luxurious than the typically utilitarian fare of the past several decades. Adding first-class spa facilities within hotel walls was the next logical step. (And who can be surprised that an increasing number of spa guests are men? The stigma of a luxurious and spirit-inducing treatment being somehow unmanly has been circling the drain for some time now.)

What a happy coincidence that this phenomenon has conflated with an explosion of creativity that is unparalleled in the hotel industry. The past 25 years has produced a pantheon of designers whose work continues to set the bar. From pioneer firms (HBA/Hirsch Bedner Associates) to today's firebrands (Richardson Sadeki), great design has planted seeds in very welcoming ground. Has the culture ever been more design-conscious than it is today? Television shows and magazines whose purpose is to make consumers savvy and proactive about their physical environments abound. The result, for hotels—even for many mid-range properties—is a challenge to meet guest expectations when the guest is no longer willing to tolerate the ordinary.

Such creative fecundity in hotel design allows the spa designer striking latitude to create environments at once soothing, beautiful, and imaginative—pleasure palaces where the mind relaxes and the spirit soars.

Bathhouse Spa at The Hotel

The Hotel is a purposeful antidote to the giant theme hotels (think: King Tut, King Arthur, Kings County) that define Las Vegas, Nevada, USA. However nestled within the large water-themed Mandalay Bay Resort and Casino, The Hotel has a separate entrance, its own lounge and café, and a distinctive vibe. The all-suite hotel has an upscale, sophisticated design that you'd expect to find in a boutique establishments in New York City or San Francisco. The dramatic, art-filled lobby leads you to the breathtaking Bathhouse Spa on the second floor, where the goal is to bring you balance, beauty, and bliss.

The stairway to the mezzanine at Bathhouse Spa at The Hotel crosses a rock-lined water trough
Photos: Andrew Bordwin

New York City-based Richardson Sadeki creates a modern spa with drama and artfulness. The architects arrange 13 treatment rooms, wet and dry lounges, pools, private tubs, steam rooms, and saunas within 15,000 square feet (1,390 square meters) of multi-dimensional space made mostly of black slate and glass. Upon your arrival through monumental smooth-textured stone walls, you journey through a canyon of rough-hewn slate and illuminated water. Water is a major theme of the design, which draws inspiration from the traditional Roman spa experience, and appears as decorative streams and rainfalls, as well as in therapeutic soaking tubs, steam rooms, and plunge pools. The interplay between privacy and openness is brought out by the combination of free-flowing space and various degrees of transparency in glass doors and partitions. Contrasting light and dark also contributes to this interplay, with the deep slate giving way to brighter white in the locker, vanity, and treatment areas. This very contemporary design is warm and welcoming—and all encompassing, as the designers, who helped develop the concept for the spa, also created Bathhouse's corporate identity, retail packaging, and uniforms.

How could you go to Bathhouse and not partake of a bath itself? Calming, Herbal, Floral, and Mud concoctions highlight Bathhouse Baths, as do Asian ingredients, such as invigorating Chai Tea and soothing Green Tea. Many of Bathhouse's ingredients for scrubs and lotions sound like they belong on your shopping list, and make for delicious treatments. There are Yummy Scrubs of chocolate and cappuccino, as well as a Crème Brûlée Body Wrap. Other scrubs and wraps use milk, honey, cinnamon, honeydew, almonds, raw cane sugar, carrots, sour cherries, pumpkins, parsley, cucumbers, wild plums, and tomatoes. You can even do the Create-Your-Own Body Wrap by choosing a body polish, body masque, and moisturizer from a long list of luscious options. Several modalities—massage, facial, scrub, and wrap—employ Hot 'n' Cold methods of combining stimulating ingredients and temperatures with heat applications. After a long day of sightseeing (or standing by the craps tables) give yourself a Blue Corn and Avocado Mani/Pedi with blue-corn soak and scrub, fresh olive oil application, and avocado mask and lotion. And, since you're in Vegas, where the rich and famous come to play, be sure to partake in the Champagne Body Wrap and the Caviar Facial.

The seductive spa is on the second floor of The Hotel

Above: Hot pools and clear surfaces give a meditative atmosphere
Right: Free-flowing floor plan leads to pools and lounges

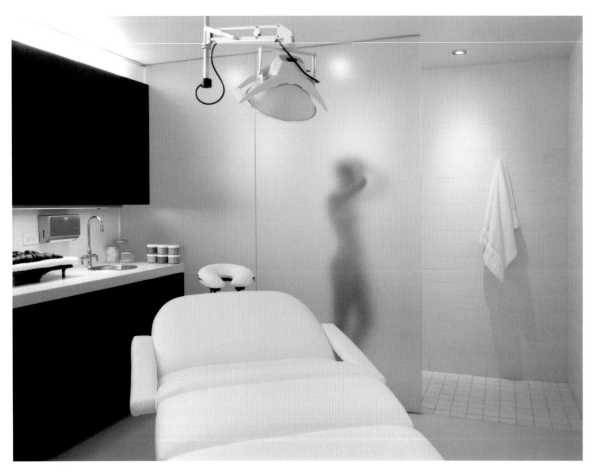

Left: Treatment rooms are spare and contemporary
Right: Locker rooms are lined with articulated white stone

Top: Rough-hewn slate, glass, and water are the dominant design materials
Above: Layered spaces play on themes of intimacy and openness

Sámas at Park Hotel Kenmare

The Park Hotel Kenmare in Kerry, Ireland, dates from 1897. Kenmare is a planned town founded in 1670 that still maintains many of its original features. Named Kerry's first Heritage Town, scenic Kenmare lies at the foot of the Cork and Kerry mountains in southwest Ireland. The Park Hotel overlooks picturesque Kenmare Bay, and offers tennis, croquet, and garden walks on its grounds. Nearby are golf courses, horseback riding stables, and fishing opportunities. The hotel prides itself on personal service, concentrating on the guests in its 46 rooms that are beautifully furnished with antiques; thus there are no meeting facilities to draw the staff's attention away from guests. There is, of course, the spa called Sámas, which means "indulgence of the senses" in Gaelic.

You'll commune with nature in the infinity-edge pool at Park Hotel Kenmare's Sámas spa
Photos: courtesy Park Hotel Kenmare

Situated in a wooden knoll, Sámas brings you closer to the surrounding beauty of nature. Oppermann Associates Architects of Dublin contrasts the hotel's history with a crisp, contemporary design for the 10,000-square-foot (930-square-meter) spa. Light and dark woods, lacquered surfaces, ashlar stone, and earth-toned tile help bring the feeling of refined nature indoors. These themes start in the lobby, which affords views of the woods through a broad expanse of glass. The heart of Sámas is the sprawling relaxation and pool area, a series of indoor and outdoor rooms at the cusp of a wooded glen. Relaxation lounges are equipped with ergonomic daybeds and your choice of music through noise-reduction headphones. Under a slatted canopy of wood and metal, the outdoor infinity-edge vitality pool faces the bay. Body, foot, and neck massage are featured in the vitality pool, where you can gaze on the views while reclining on a therapeutic aqua bench.

Trinity being an intrinsic concept to the Irish, the ethos of Sámas is three-part: thermal suite, holistic treatment, pure relaxation. Instead of specific services, you can simply reserve a time and then consult with your therapist about the most appropriate treatments while you enjoy a welcoming Foot Ritual. Rock sauna, aroma steam, and laconium fulfill the thermal aspect to Sámas' mission, while various modalities address the needs of your body, mind, and soul. For women, Anam ("the soul") is a back, face, and scalp treatment with deep cleansing and exfoliation, followed by massage with aromatic oils and hot stones. Finish with an acupressure facial. The lads enjoy Fe ("to calm"), a combination experience of reflexology, hot-stone massage, calming facial, and scalp massage. The tai chi pavilion offers sessions in that ancient art of movement, as well as in yoga, meditation, and Pilates. Morning Serenity Walks guide you through the nature trails of Kenmare, as you awaken to all the senses that you have so beautifully indulged.

Left: Ergonomic loungers face the woods and bay
Right: Tai chi and other movement workshops bring you serenity

Left: A series of indoor and outdoor rooms houses lounges and pools
Right: Vitality pool features a therapeutic aqua bench and water jets

Estrella Spa at Viceroy Palm Springs

Nothing is cooler these days than the desert of Palm Springs, California, USA. Estrella Spa at Viceroy Palm Springs lies at the base of the San Jacinto Mountains, near downtown. Weekenders of all ages are enjoying the resurgence of Hollywood's playground, just two quick hours from Los Angeles. Known as an enclave of Mid-Century Modernism, Palm Springs also boasts pre-war structures, such as the one housing the Viceroy hotel. Originally unveiled in 1933, the boutique hotel known then as Estrella was popular—then as it is again—with Hollywood folk. A recent redesign added 15 villas, event and meeting center, fitness pavilion and spa, indoor/outdoor yoga pavilion, and lap pool, which results in a mannered, sophisticated getaway. Amid manicured courtyards with cypress trees, topiaries, and palms are 74 rooms—either studios, suites or individual villas—most with private terrace or patio. Two adult-only pools and one family pool accommodate all types of guests.

Lemony yellow accents the crisp black and white palette of Estrella Spa at Viceroy Palm Springs
Photos: Grey Crawford

Creating a modern take on the Regency style that was popular during Hollywood's golden age, Los Angeles-based Kelly Wearstler Interior Design (KWID) uses a crisp palette of black, white, and yellow. Classical forms, seen in planters and lamps modeled after Greek pottery, mix with the indoor/outdoor ambiance that defines Palm Springs. Coachman's lamps, formal drapery, white whippet dog statues, and draped pavilions exude a formality that is softened by their tongue-in-cheek theatrical quality. Bold Greek-key patterns flow along room and outdoor drapes, and morph into the graphic "e" logo of Estrella Spa, which was named to honor the heritage of the original hotel. Black-and-white patterns in wallpaper and upholstery are accented by bright yellow accessories in the lounge, where you can relax by the fire and sip tea-based tonics. The spa includes a fitness center with yoga, tai chi, and Pilates areas. Treatment and massage rooms are decorated in the graphic color combinations, while locker rooms and wet areas are covered floor-to-ceiling in white beveled tile with black accents. Four outdoor massage cabanas bring you into the desert air.

Estrella's signature treatments are designed to relax and revitalize you. Citrus Ylang-Ylang Body Wrap exfoliates with a warm oil wrap, foot massage, aromatic oils, and shea butter moisturizer. Using techniques developed in Japan, Estrella Bamboo Ritual is an aromatic journey that starts with cleansing algae, exfoliating bamboo-ginger scrub, soothing rice packs, and moisturizing plum lotion, all of which is worked deeply into your skin by shiatsu massage. A novel combination is the Yoga Facial, which combines yoga's inner-body benefits with aesthetic enhancements that relieve facial-muscle tension through massage and exfoliation with stretching motions and acupressure. Your often-overlooked limbs get pampered during a Revitalizing Hand and Arm Treatment that uses invigorating hot-towel compresses, loofah exfoliation, and massage, as well as with the Nurturing Foot and Leg Treatment, which gives you a curative botanical foot soak, sea-salt exfoliation, and rhythmic massage. Whether using organic seaweed, self-heating mud, or indigenous minerals, Estrella Spa is your true oasis in the desert.

Top left to right:
Massage rooms exude bygone Hollywood style
Greek-inspired classical touches are seen in the lamps and accessories
Black and white form the color palette
Right: Statue whippets stand at attention throughout the manicured lawns

The Spa at Mandarin Oriental, New York

The multi-use Time Warner Center in New York City, USA, is home to Mandarin Oriental, New York, on the 35th through 54th floors of the building at Columbus Circle on Central Park South, designed by Skidmore, Owings & Merrill. In addition to the 250-room hotel, the Center houses CNN's production studios, offices, luxury retail, restaurants, and a jazz performance hall. Beginning at the hotel's entrance, you experience an atmosphere of rare beauty and craft. The lobby is illuminated by a dramatic ceiling fixture made of Waterford crystal by noted glass artist Dale Chihuly. Marble, mosaic, and tooled metals create more sparkle in the public areas. The Asian influence is strongly seen in two dominant guestroom color schemes of pale gold/jet black and Chinese red/sterling silver. Furnishings inspired by the 1940s complete the look of urban sophistication. Views of Central Park and the city skyline are at every turn at the Mandarin Oriental, which strives to combine aesthetics and atmosphere of both Asia and New York. What better place to do that than the 14,500-square-foot (1,345-square-meter) spa and fitness center dedicated to holistic rejuvenation?

Mandarin Oriental, New York, is part of the Time Warner Center
Photos: George Apostolidis

The global hospitality design firm HBA/Hirsch Bedner Associates' Atlanta, Georgia, USA, office—along with New York City-based Brennan Beer Gorman Architects—extends the design of the hotel public and guestroom areas to the serene spa. It's designed to impart a sense of unreality by using sparkling silver leaf, glass mosaic tile, diaphanous fabrics, natural stone, and Japanese rice paper. A stone-encrusted water feature adds calm to the lounge area. Bamboo flooring and other light woods combine with crisp white fabrics for a clean and meditative look. Eight private treatment rooms have views to the city and the park, and display Asian themes in the rice-paper-lined doors and bento-box-like cabinetry. A sumptuous VIP suite is decorated with traditional Chinese furniture and fabrics, and includes its own thermarium, steam, sauna, fireplace, and changing room. The 25-yard (23-meter) lap pool runs parallel to the Hudson River, which is seen through large picture windows.

The Spa at Mandarin Oriental, New York, has a full slate of modalities to relax you, in addition to its stone-lined vitality pool and sparkling amethyst crystal steam room. Customized Time Rituals are designed to restore your equilibrium, and are performed in sequence to welcome, purify, nurture, and balance, resulting in a blissful you. Based on ancient techniques of Chinese, ayurvedic, European, Balinese, and Thai cultures, the ritual experiences combine body scrub and wrap with body and head massage for detoxifying, toning, relaxing, stress relief, immunity boosting, energizing, or jet lag recovery. To soften your skin, Honey, Sesame, and Green Tea Scrub makes use of the ingredients' natural beneficial enzymes and vitamins. Your body wrap might use marine mud or algae, or Oshadi clay mixed with ginger, licorice, and mustard seed. Dosha-specific ayurvedic wraps are available, depending on your needs: Vata Comforter for dry skin gives you nourishment and comfort; Pitta Pacifier for sensitive skin calms overactive minds and bodies; and Kapha Stimulator for dull skin purifies and improves circulation. The signature Life Dance Massage begins with a welcoming foot cleanse, then continues with skin softening sea salt and essential oil scrub, a gentle facial, and then the shiatsu-inspired free-flowing massage, concluding with an Oriental Head Massage that brings you to the desired state of blissful serenity.

Top left: Traditional Chinese bed highlights the spa VIP suite
Top right: Silver leaf and Japanese rice paper add Asian touches to treatment rooms
Above: Lap pool runs parallel to the Hudson River espied through the windows

Left: Vitality pool is bathed in both natural and artificial light
Above: Amethyst crystal steam room sparkles with beauty and health

Kara at Park Hyatt Los Angeles

Named for the Greek word for "purity," Kara is a place of pure pleasure and relaxation at the Park Hyatt on the Avenue of the Stars in Century City, a business and entertainment center in Los Angeles, California, USA. The word Kara also has associations of joy and being at the pinnacle, so it makes sense that Hyatt Hotels would reserve this spa for its premium brand of Park Hyatt. Catering mostly to business travelers, Park Hyatt Los Angeles underwent a $20-million renovation, which included adding sumptuous marble baths and softly contemporary wood furniture to its 366 guestrooms.

Kara's private spa villas are oriented toward Park Hyatt Los Angeles' garden
Photo: Jennifer Boggs

Space and privacy are pure luxuries, and those are the guiding forces behind Kara's design concept by HCA Design of Toronto, Ontario, Canada. The 11,220-square-foot (1,040-square-meter) spa on the second floor of the hotel comprises three individual spa villas, each with a meditative garden. Before you are escorted to these private oases, you will arrive at the warmly contemporary maple and marble entry, whose curved fire-toned wall embraces you. Here, you'll begin to relax with a cup of signature Kara tea. The reception area also affords you ready access to the 16-foot-long (4.8-meter) manicure bar, the pedicure thrones, and the garden. Reminiscent of gardens in southeast Polynesia, this spa garden is a transitional space, with teak flooring, horsetail bamboo plantings, and cushioned cedar chairs. From there, you will luxuriate in a 680-square-foot (63-square-meter) treatment villa with relaxation lounge, shower, vanity area, and deep soaking tub equipped with chromo therapy. In a purely delightful touch, the tubs are filled by a steady stream of water flowing from a ceiling-mounted fixture. You can also laze on the built-in body-shaped lounge space, and watch television or listen to a variety of soothing music from your individually controlled sound system.

Begin your escape to purity with the Kara Welcome Ritual, a cleansing footbath and a soothing foot treatment in the tranquillity garden to help you release stress and prepare for your experience. Upon entering your private spa villa, the temperature, lighting, and music will be adjusted to meet your individual preferences. Signature Aromasoul Massages come in the choice of Oriental (Chinese meridian stimulation), Mediterranean (peaceful, fluid strokes), Indian (energy balancing), or Arabian (calming). A Thermofreeze Anti-Cellulite Intense Wrap increases metabolism and circulation with a series of hot and cold applications. For the total experience, go on one of Kara's Escapes, a series of massage, facial, and body treatment geared toward Tranquillity, Purity, Energy, Harmony, or New Life for expectant mothers. There's also a Teen Renewal Escape with acne-fighting tropical algae facial, make-up lesson, and manicure, and Jet Set Escapes that Relax (with botanical facial and Arabian Aromasoul Massage) or Restore (with anti-oxidant facial and Mediterranean Aromasoul Massage). Facials of every sort are available to oxygenate, rebalance, purify, refresh, nourish, renew, redefine, revitalize, hydrate, and illuminate your skin with the use of essential oils, clay, algae, antioxidants, soy proteins, alpha-hydroxy acids, collagen, honey, and pearl powder. For the ultimate experience, indulge in a 90-minute facial that is a combination of Absolute Pearl and Glorious Skin Treatments to add smoothness, firmness, tone, lightness, and luminosity to face, neck, and sexy décolletage. It's called the Red Carpet Radiance Facial, of course, as you'd expect on the Avenue of the Stars!

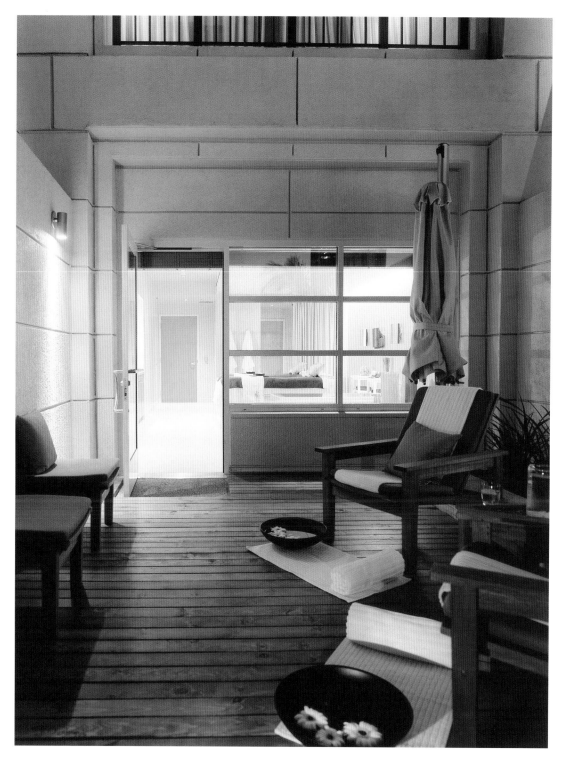

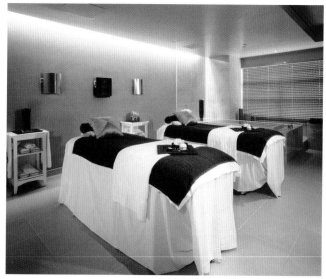

Above: Spacious spa villas have their own Polynesian-inspired garden. Photo: Jennifer Boggs

Above: Your feet—and soul—will be pampered as you arrive to the tranquillity garden. Photo: Henry Cabala
Opposite top: Light, sound, and temperature are individually controlled for your comfort. Photo: Henry Cabala
Opposite middle: Oversized soaking tub is filled by flowing water from above. Photo: Henry Cabala
Opposite bottom: Built-in lounger is body shaped for pure relaxation. Photo: Patrick Messina

Quality Spa and Resort Holmsbu

Barely an hour from Oslo, Norway, in a bay between Holmsbu and Rødtangen, is the charming Quality Spa and Resort Holmsbu. The small, picturesque town offers you shops and coffee houses when you're not experiencing a spa treatment or the many water activities on the bay. Quality Spa is full service, with a conference center, and a private boat landing for guests who prefer that mode of transportation and recreation. You also have the choice of both indoor and outdoor swimming pools and whirlpools, which are enjoyed year round.

Above: Cabins at Quality Spa and Resort Holmsbu are 13 feet (4 meters) above the water
Right: Mezzanine overlooks indoor pool
Photos: Christen Ræstad

Perched along the bay are 183 guest rooms, 131 of which are in traditional cottages and cabins by the water. Architecture firm Halvorsen of Drammen, Norway, rests a series of cottages on the small slope overlooking the bay, while it places cabins 13 feet (four meters) above the water surface. The maritime environment is heightened even more by the variety of board-and-batten construction and shingled roofs in crimson and blue. Team Interioret Hanne Hovland, interior designer from Oslo, Norway, creates a design scheme of light mahogany, cream, and crisp white furniture in the Scandinavian style. The outdoor pool area is surrounded by a wooden deck, while the outdoor, communal whirlpool rests on one of the sodded decks. Spa areas and 12 treatment rooms are crisp and contemporary with stone, tile, and wood. Square cut-outs on the floor of the mezzanine afford views to the indoor pool below. A traditional sauna overlooks the active fjord.

The Quality Spa aims to impart health and knowledge to you in its menu of treatments that service your well-being. Facials freshen, firm, and smooth the skin, especially the intense Vitamin and Mineral Bomb, whose combination of high-power vitamin C and dry, frozen algae is especially good at combating effects of the sun. Also for sun worshippers is the Water Lily Wrap that cools sun-damaged skin with fragrant water lily for moisture and green tea for repair. Treatments are given expressive names, such as Goodbye Baggy Eyes, Without a Straw, and One Less Number, which treats your swollen feet to a footbath with aromatic oils, followed by a stimulating massage and foot mask. Desert Sand Body Wrap gives you an uplifting feeling with a mix of mineral-rich desert sand, while Nirvana Massage drips you with running, warm oils. For a treatment that's closer to the water, try the Ocean Cleansing Feast, where applications and wraps of warm algae mixtures connect you to the bay city of Holmsbu.

Top: Steam room is decorated with mosaic tile
Left: Outdoor pool resembles large soaking tub with overflow edge

Spa at Las Ventanas al Paraiso

At the tip of Mexico's Baja Peninsula, along the coast of the Sea of Cortez, lay the "windows to paradise"—Las Ventanas al Paraiso. True to its name, this exquisite location is in an area of Los Cabos, Mexico, that is less traveled than the typical tourist spots. Your trip to paradise begins as you are personally received, then escorted to your room, one of 61 residential-type suites, each with ocean or golf-course view, private terrace, and splash/whirlpool. A serpentine network of ponds and pools brings you to the generous beachfront infinity-edge pool that features a swim-up bar with in-water stools. Local seafood and organic ingredients comprise the inventive menus offered at the Sea Grill, The Restaurant, and the Cava wine cellar. Nature is all around you, from the azure Sea of Cortez and the verdant desert landscape of the 18-hole golf course, to the starry heavens above espied through the hotel's large computerized telescope or your personal one in your suite.

Serpentine pool wraps around various lounging areas at Las Ventanas al Paraiso
Photos: courtesy Las Ventanas al Paraiso

The connection to water and nature is paramount in the design by noted hotel interior designers Wilson & Associates of Dallas, Texas, USA. The resort blends into the natural environment, hugging the upward slope of the terrain. Landscaping uses locally found boulders, rocks, and flowering plants, while interiors in earthy pastel colors with natural wood and stone maintain a connection to the land. The design and architecture relate to traditional Mexican forms and materials, such as cedar, iron, and stucco. Native latilla screens of peeled sticks are formed over patios for beautifully filtered sunlight effects, and are applied to interior ceilings for a continued outdoor feeling. Art from Mexican artists is seen throughout public and private spaces, and the traditional work of local artisans and crafters is emphasized through mosaics (the illusory stone carpets), hand-painted ceramics, and intricate ironwork, for which Mexico is famous. Guest suites are created as mini residences in a free-flowing layout. Carved cedar doors, hand-crafted furniture, and pebble-inlay headboards in sunburst designs exude welcoming beauty. For the spa, a garden ambiance is found in the treatment rooms, some with sliding cedar doors opening to private gardens. Others are adorned with soothing water walls and hand-painted murals. Separate garden courtyards for men and women give you access to sauna, steam, whirlpool, and cold plunge. In addition to the treatment rooms, you may enjoy services at the beachside pavilion, in your suite, or on one of the hotel yachts available for charter.

Enlarging on the connection you'll make with the nature around you, ingredients that take you to paradise are local aloe vera, sage, lavender, elephant tree, cactus, chaparral, and tree tobacco. Signature treatments rely on ancient indigenous Mexican cures, such as nopal cactus, eucalyptus, and volcanic clay. The Nopal Anti-Cellulite and Detox Wrap takes its power from the native nopal cactus, a source of vitamin C and amino acids, and works on fluid retention through a nopal gel cocoon, nopal lotion massage, and a nopal-pineapple smoothie that you'll enjoy at the end of the treatment. Desert Healer's anti-bacterial medicinal bath of sage, elephant tree, eucalyptus, and chaparral eliminates toxins through your pores while delivering strong anti-oxidant results, as does the pineapple-chaparral tincture you'll imbibe for continued cleansing inside and out. With Desert Purification, you will be swathed in the same clays that Aztecs and Mayans used in their ritual purification. Adding a luxurious touch, you'll follow the exfoliation with a juniper-sage massage oil application and a sauna. The Desert Flower—Soothing the Feminine experience begins with your skin exfoliated with sea salt, damiana, sage, desert lavender, wild yam, and red raspberry leaves, then a float in a bath of aromatic herbs, followed by massage with desert-herb oils so you emerge fresh as the desert bloom for which this signature treatment is named.

Top left: Infinity-edge pool blends into the Sea of Cortez
Top right: Gardens and patios lead you to the expansive pool deck
Left: Spa entrance features boulders culled from the site

Top left: Rough stucco is accented by authentic Mexican ironwork
Top right: Mexican crafters create stone "rugs" throughout the hotel
Right: Treatment rooms open up to private garden idylls

The Oriental Spa at The Oriental, Bangkok

For the past 30 of its almost 130 years of existence, The Oriental, Bangkok, in Thailand, has been owned and managed by Mandarin Oriental Hotel Group, which considers this—its second property—a flagship in the Group's impressive, world-wide empire. The hotel's history includes accommodating such noted writers as Joseph Conrad and Noel Coward. Located just across the Chao Phya River from the almost 400-room legendary hotel is The Oriental Spa, a consistently top-rated temple of well-being. Visited by political and cultural dignitaries, the spa artfully blends ancient Thai and modern western techniques in a wide variety of treatments performed in the 14 private spa suites.

A colonial house is home to The Oriental Spa at The Oriental, Bangkok
Photo: George Apostolidis

Bangkok-based architect L'Atelier 10 joined with interior designer Morford & Company of Hong Kong to create the beautifully detailed spa nestled within a colonial-style house. The dramatic, double-height entrance sets the tone with a serene lily pond and illuminating whiteness. All treatments are performed in private suites that flow with tactile teak wood used for floors, walls, furniture, and artfully carved partitions for a dual sense of openness and privacy. Thai accents and other traditional décor elements belie state-of-the-art hydrotubs, saunas, and shower systems. Nonetheless, spa equipment is kept to a minimum, with floor mattresses giving a more elemental feeling than a raised massage bed might. Soaking tubs offer an authentic Asian experience. A large yoga and meditation room is kept spare and simple, in keeping with the transformative modalities practiced in the space.

Meditation, massage, and natural herbal remedies based on ancient medical knowledge are the hallmarks of the treatment array at The Oriental. Fragrant oils, aromatic herbs, and luscious fruit and vegetable extracts combine for the range of body and facial treatments, which you may enjoy à la carte, or indulge in during half-, full-, or three-day programs. Protein-rich massage oils of sesame, olive, and citronella are combined with herbs to cleanse and stimulate your skin and muscles, especially in the Jet Lag Recovery Treatment. Signature Oriental Body Glow features an exclusive mixture of mint, lavender, and other seeds and flowers from the hills of northern Thailand. Combined with honey, the exfoliants increase circulation, making you glow, while the honey nourishes your skin for a soft and smooth feeling. Communing with the healing properties of water is Essence of Aqua, a four-stage treatment that begins with body scrub on a heated marble table followed by hydro-massage and then body masque with seaweed, mud, Thai herbs, and organic black sticky rice that is absorbed by the skin in the rhassoul steam chamber. The final stage is a light massage with a soothing body lotion to complete your top-rated experience at The Oriental.

Left: Entrance is bathed in light from above
Right: Carved teak screens impart both privacy and openness.
Opposite left: Deluxe spa suite features multi-headed state-of-the-art shower
Photos: Robert Hubel

Top right: Yoga and meditation are practiced in a teak-clad room
Right: Flower-strewn soaking tub highlights the Oriental suite
Photos: George Apostolidis

Spa Bellagio

Truly the gold standard of mega-hotels that line the famous Strip of Las Vegas, Nevada, USA, Bellagio is a major presence in a place where every square inch fights for attention. The 3,000-room hotel was designed by The Jerde Partnership International of Los Angeles, California, USA, which modeled it after villas around Italy's Lake Como. Bellagio's world-famous dancing fountains are choreographed to music ranging from opera to rock. Things aquatic again meet your eye as you enter the vast lobby with its mesmerizing, water-themed sculpture by American glass artist Dale Chihuly.

Spa Bellagio is a highlight of the famous Las Vegas hotel
Photos: Robert Mora

Keeping current, Spa Bellagio recently underwent a renovation by Las Vegas-based architect and interior designer Marnell Corrao Associates. The 65,000-square-foot (6,040-square-meter) spa, salon, and fitness center is designed based on natural philosophies of Zen, balancing elements of earth (granite, shellstone), water (water walls, watsu), fire (candles), and wind (fans). Clean lines and natural materials, such as travertine, bleached walnut, and onyx, set a meditative tone, along with jade and hand-blown glass accents. Catering to high-rollers, Spa Bellagio makes a concerted effort to address the needs of its male patrons with private barber room and relaxation balcony overlooking the hotel pool. Again, water is a defining element seen in reflecting pools, water walls, and illuminated aqua-colored glass. Water walls inserted with glowing candles set the mood in the meditation room.

With a global clientele, Spa Bellagio looks to Hindu, Chinese, and European techniques. Ashiatsu Oriental Bar Therapy, an ancient bodywork method using deep compression, is performed while a barefoot therapist holds onto bars attached to the ceiling. For a lighter touch, drops of nine pure essential oils are applied in Raindrop Therapy along your spine, followed by hot towels to infuse the oils deep into your body. A separate area for watsu underwater massage can accommodate couples for a simultaneous experience. Green Coffee Contour Treatment uses phyto-extracts found naturally in green coffee to provide smoothing and contouring, while Cooling Eye Therapy turns to aquamarine stones that are placed over soothing eye compresses filled with chamomile. Even if you didn't make a killing at the casino, you can still be a winner at the spa, where you'll be swathed in riches with the Egyptian Gold Body Treatment of ritualistic exfoliation, hydrating gel wrap, and multi-action oil application that concludes with a dusting of real gold.

Top left: Italianate garden motifs enhance the pool area
Top right: Therapist walks on your back during Ashiatsu Oriental Bar Therapy
Right: Zen elements of earth, water, and fire come together in the hot tub area

Spa Without Walls at The Fairmont Orchid

For total freedom and connection with site, the Spa Without Walls at The Fairmont Orchid is the Big Kahuna. Situated on the Kohala Coast of the Big Island of Hawaii, USA, the beautiful beachfront property spans 32 acres (13 hectares), and has 540 guest rooms and suites. The Big Island's range of flora and fauna encompasses majestic palm trees, tropical rainforests, and the Hawaiian green sea turtles that visit the Fairmont's beach each afternoon. Outrigger canoeing, cultural hikes, Hawaiian crafts, snorkeling in Pauoa Bay, and golfing on lava-based greens are island activities for you and your family. Or, of course, you can always lounge by the 10,000-square-foot (930-square-meter) oceanfront pool or soak in the lava whirlpools.

Island breezes and scents of the sea highlight Spa Without Walls' oceanfront pavilion experience at The Fairmont Orchid
Photos: Wally Krysciak

The concept of a Spa Without Walls is to immerse you in the beautiful outdoor surroundings that Honolulu, Hawaii-based hospitality architecture firm Wimberly Allison Tong & Goo is highly familiar with. You'll await your treatment in teak loungers on outdoor terraces that dot the landscape. Ten island-inspired massage hales (houses) are nestled among a flowing network of waterfalls, streams, lily ponds, and lava rock formations, while five cabanas dot the oceanfront. Native woven laubala (pandanus or screwpine leaves) covers the walls of wooden hales, while roll-up bamboo blinds control how much exposure you have. All around you is the tropical landscape of orchids, banana trees, coconut palms, native laua'e, and hapu'u tree ferns. Two puka (window) hales are cantilevered over ponds with windows beneath the tables to give you a view of swimming koi. Six indoor treatment rooms are also available in the spa center, where you'll find steam and sauna areas and a resting lounge.

Massage and body treatments are infused with natural healing ingredients from Hawaii, such as medicinal plants used in the Hawaiian Revitalizer Wrap. The signature Big Island Vanilla Coffee Exfoliation uses an aromatic scrub with crushed organic Kona coffee beans and orange lotion to exfoliate your skin, then continues with vanilla-lotion massage. Lomi lomi is the traditional Hawaiian massage modality, which uses rhythmic strokes of the forearm for deep muscle massage. You can learn this and other techniques in the Art of Massage sessions for couples, with time to practice on each other. A wide range of Chinese therapies is available, including acupressure (manual stimulation of pressure points), acupuncture (needle insertion at specific body areas), moxibustion (herb burning at pressure points), cupping (detox with suction cups), and personalized Chinese herb mixtures given to you in pill, tea, tincture, or powder form. There's also personalized yoga instruction and health walks through ancient lava flows and rainforests without walls.

Above: Hotel and spa are perched on the Kohala Coast, protected by five sacred mountains
Right: Majestic palms frame the entry to the hotel

Above: The expansive pool area is for swimming, lounging, and dining

The Spa at Four Seasons Resort Chiang Mai

The lush Mae Rim Valley is the setting for The Spa at Four Seasons Resort Chiang Mai in Chiang Mai, located in northern Thailand. Landscaped gardens, two small lakes, lily ponds, streams, and waterfalls spread throughout 20 acres (8 hectares) of land, which includes a terraced working rice farm that hosts a family of water buffalo. Inspired by the 700-year-old Lanna (Northern) Kingdom of Thailand, Four Seasons Chiang Mai is planned as a traditional village. Seventy plush suites exude a refined Asian atmosphere and afford views of the gardens from outdoor living areas.

The sacred bo tree—a symbol of enlightenment—is a decorative motif throughout The Spa at Four Seasons Resort Chiang Mai. Photo: Luca Tettoni

The 9,685-square-foot (900-square-meter) spa is designed in the ancient Lanna style by Bunnag Architects of Bangkok, Thailand. Inspired by Thai temples, the three-story, shingle-roof building features hand-carved wooden screens. As you glide through the space, you'll come to indoor rooms spilling to semi-enclosed terraces with soaking tubs and outdoor showers. Rich tones of maroon and gold (used in the Lanna era to depict the sun) cover walls and furnishings of seven spacious treatment suites, five boasting private herbal aromatherapy steam rooms, and two with double rain-shower massage beds. The Laan Chang penthouse treatment suite takes up the entire top floor, and has double semi-outdoor shower, herbal steam, Thai and Western massage beds, outdoor soaking tub, and private sala (covered gazebo), all overlooking the dramatic Doi Suthep Doi Pui mountain range. Throughout the indoor and outdoor spaces, a stylized leaf from the sacred bo tree (Buddha learned his principles under one) adorns archways, walls, and sculpture.

Thai culture is stressed by the bo-leaf motif, music wafting through the halls, and ancient Thai spa rituals using herbs, spices, and aromatic oils. Thai Herbal Steam Aromatherapy was once available only in sacred temples under the guidance of monks. Now, you can enjoy the benefits of distilled combinations of Thai herb essences diffused with steam—lemongrass de-stresses, wild lime improves breathing, bai nart sage soothes muscles, morning glory clears sinuses, and prai ginger moisturizes skin. For a more intense experience, there are Herbal Aromatic Retreats, each including herbal pack and massage, followed by an elixir to imbibe. For the Romance Retreat, you'll have serenity herbal steam pack with jasmine, dok jan, and mandarin paired with a ylang-ylang oil massage, and the tropical blend of hibiscus and lemongrass tea. The Rejuvenator offers a muscle tension steam pack of greenbriar, rosemary, and cinnamon followed by an Oriental blend massage, and fruit and spice tea with ginger and rosehips. To keep on going, you can have the Energizer's jetlag steam pack of thyme, mint, and basil, get an invigorating traditional Thai massage, and sip scent-of-the-forest tea with mulberry leaves, pine, and mint. Treatments for your tresses include Wild Lime Hair Care that applies freshly crushed Thai wild limes to your hair and scalp, after which follows shampoo and conditioner with the luster-restoring essential oil of wild lime, a treatment that makes you as lush and radiant as the surrounding landscape.

Left to right:
Three-story spa is modeled after ancient temples
Outdoor living areas bring you closer to the tropical gardens
The verdant Mae Rim landscape is lush with beauty
Photos: Robert Miller

Above: Outdoor soaking tub affords views of gardens. Photo: Luca Tettoni
Opposite: Guest suites are adorned with maroon and sacred gold. Photo: Robert Miller

Above: Serene swimming pool looks out to the Northern Thai mountain range. Photo: Robert Miller
Opposite: Terraces are beautiful spaces for contemplation. Photo: Luca Tettoni

Directory

Ajune
1294 Third Avenue, New York, NY, USA;
+1 212 628 0044; www.ajune.com
Design: Robert D. Henry Architects,
New York, NY, USA; +1 212 533 4145;
www.rdh-architects.com
Photos: Dan Bibb, New York,
NY, USA; +1 212 228 0103

Amanjena Health and Beauty Center
Route de Ouarzazate,
km 12, Marrakech, Morocco;
+212 4 440 3353; www.amanresorts.com
Design: Design Realization, Paris, France;
+33 1 4222 6577

Banyan Tree Hotels & Resorts
www.banyantreespa.com
Banyan Tree Bintan: Site A4, Lagoi,
Bintan Island, Indonesia;
+62 770 693 100
Banyan Tree Seychelles: Anse Intendance,
Mahé, Republic of Seychelles;
+248 383 500
Banyan Tree Shanghai: 88 Henan Central Rd.,
Shanghai, China; +86 21 6335 1888
Architecture: Architrave Design & Planning,
Singapore; +65 6049 5888
Interiors (Bintan): H.L. Lim & Associates,
Singapore; +65 6227 2872

Bathhouse Spa at The Hotel
3950 Las Vegas Boulevard South,
Las Vegas, NV, USA; +1 702 632 7777;
www.mandalaybay.com
Design: Richardson Sadeki, New York,
NY, USA; +1 212 966 0900;
www.richardsonsadeki.com
Architecture: Klai Juba, Las Vegas, NV, USA
(architect of record); +1 707 221 2254
Photos: Andrew Bordwin, New York, NY, USA;
+1 212 627 9519; www.bordwin.com

Blue Lagoon
Vikurbraut 506, Svartsengi, Iceland;
+354 420 8800; www.bluelagoon.com
Design: VA Architects, Reykjavik, Iceland;
+354 530 6990; www.vaarkitektar.is
Photos: Haukur Snorrason, Iceland;
+354 553 7741

Blue Medical Beauty Spa
14622 Ventura Boulevard, Sherman Oaks, CA,
USA; +1 818 783 3600;
www.experienceblue.com
Design: Michael Marquez Architects,
Los Angeles, CA, USA; +1 310 447 6144;
www.mmarchitectsLA.com
Photos: Ayola Photography,
Los Angeles, CA, USA;
+1 818 885 8402; www.ayola.com

The Carneros Inn
4048 Sonoma Highway, Napa, CA, USA;
+1 707 299 4900; www.thecarnerosinn.com
Architecture: William Rawn Associates,
Boston, MA, USA; +1 617 423 3470;
www.rawnarch.com
Interiors: Shopworks, Napa, CA, USA;
+1 707 258 1924; www.shopworksdesign.com
Landscape: Olin Partnership, Philadelphia, PA,
USA; +1 215 440 0030; www.olinptr.com
Photos: Mark Hundley;
www.hundleyphoto.com
Art Gray, Santa Monica, CA, USA;
+1 310 450 2806

Chiva-Som International Health Resort
73/4 Petchkasem Road, Hua Hin, Prachuab
Khirikhan, Thailand; +66 3253 6536;
www.chivasom.com
Design: Syntax Group, Berkshire, UK;
+44 1 6287 89646
Photos: Pavan Bali, New Delhi, India;
+91 11 26112483

COMO Shambhala at Parrot Cay
Providenciales, Turks & Caicos Isles,
British West Indies; +1 649 946 7788;
www.shambhalaretreat.com
Architecture: Rothermel Cooke Smith,
Providenciales, Turks & Caicos Isles,
British West Indies; +1 649 946 4551;
www.rbsarchitects.com
Interiors: United Designers, London, UK;
+44 20 7357 6006

Daintree Eco Lodge and Spa
20 Daintree Road, Daintree, Queensland,
Australia; +61 7 4098 6100;
www.daintree-ecolodge.com.au
Photo: Michael Omm

Delos Spa Center
Mykonos Grand Hotel & Resort, Ayios
Yiannis, Mykonos, Greece;
+30 2 289 025555; www.mykonosgrand.gr
Architecture: Papagiannis & Associates,
Mykonos, Greece; +30 2 103 600711
Interiors: MKV Design, London, UK;
+44 20 7242 2466; www.mkvdesign.com
Photos: Demitris Poupalos, Greece;
+30 6 947 77 8754

E'SPA at Gianfranco Ferré
Via S. Andrea 15, Milan, Italy;
+39 02 76 01 75 26;
www.gianfrancoferre.com
Architecture: Ezio Riva, Milan, Italy;
+39 02 72 13 41
Interiors: Gianfranco Ferré, Milan, Italy;
+39 02 72 13 41; www.gianfrancoferre.com
Photos: Paola de Pietri, Italy;
+39 05 22 43 13 65

Estrella Spa at Viceroy Palm Springs
415 So. Belardo Road, Palm Springs,
CA, USA; +1 760 320 4117;
www.viceroypalmsprings.com
Design: Kelly Wearstler Interior Design,
Los Angeles, CA, USA; +1 323 951 7454;
www.kwid.com
Landscape: Zeitgeist Design, Florence,
AZ, USA; +1 602 332 5193
Photos: Grey Crawford, Pasadena,
CA, USA; +1 626 304 2646

Evian Spa by Three
No. 3 The Bund, 2nd Floor, 3 Zhong Shan,
Dong Yi Rd., Shanghai, China;
+86 21 6321 6622; www.threeonthebund.com
Design: Alan Chan Design Company,
Hong Kong; +852 2527 8228;
www.alanchandesign.com

The Greenhouse
127 East 57th Street, New York, NY, USA;
+1 212 644 4449;
www.thegreenhousespa.com
Design: S. Russell Groves, New York, NY, USA;
+1 212 929 5221; www.srussellgroves.com
Photos: Mark Ross, New York, NY, USA;
+1 212 744 7258

Island Spa at Kuda Huraa
Four Seasons Resort Maldives at Kuda Huraa,
North Malé Atoll, Republic of the Maldives;
+960 444 888; www.fourseasons.com
Architecture: Grounds Kent Architects,
Fremantle, Australia; +61 8 9335 7622
Interiors: Hinke Zieck, Bali, Indonesia;
+62 361 270241
Photos: Peter Mealin, Singapore;
+65 9634 6761

Kara at Park Hyatt Los Angeles
2151 Avenue of the Stars, Los Angeles,
CA, USA; +1 310 277 1234;
www.parklosangeles.hyatt.com
Design: HCA Design, Toronto, ON,
Canada; +1 416 482 5216; www.hca.ca
Photos: Jennifer Boggs, Los Angeles,
CA, USA; +1 323 906 0803
Henry Cabala, Long Beach, CA, USA;
+1 562 432 5168; www.henrycabala.com
Patrick Messina, France; +33 0612224083

Liquidrom Therme Bath
Möckernstrasse 10, Berlin, Germany;
+49 30 74737 174; www.liquidrom.com
Architecture: Architecture von Gerkan, Marg
and Partner, Hamburg, Germany;
+49 40 88151 154; www.gmp-architekten.de
Interiors: Liquid Sound, Bad Sulza, Germany;
+49 36 46192 881; www.liquiddsound.com
Photos: Linda Troeller, New York, NY, USA;
+1 212 647 9808
Christian Gahl, Germany; +49 17 77870 379

Mii amo
Enchantment Resort, 525 Boynton Canyon
Rd., Sedona, AZ, USA; +1 520 203 8500;
www.miiamo.com
Architecture: Gluckman Mayner Architects,
New York, NY; +1 212 929 0100;
www.gluckmanmayner.com
Spa Design: SPAdesign, Sedona, AZ, USA;
+1 928 204 2338
Photos: Harry Zernike, New York, NY, USA;
+1 917 324 5040; www.harryzernike.com
Eika Aoshin/Visages, Los Angeles, CA, USA;
+1 323 650 8880; www.visages.com

Miramar Crouesty
Port Crouesty, Arzon, France;
+33 2 97 53 4900;
www.miramar-crouesty.com
Design: Pierre Diener Architecture,
Paris, France; +33 1 45 74 3233
Photos: Jacques Boulay, Paris, France;
+33 1 43 48 98 92

Nemacolin Woodlands Resort and Spa
1001 LaFayette Drive, Farmington, PA, USA;
+1 724 329 8555; www.nemacolin.com
Architecture: Burt Hill Kosar Rittleman,
Pittsburgh, PA, USA; +1 412 394 7000;
www.burthill.com
Interiors: Clodagh Design International,
New York, NY, USA; +1 212 780 5300;
www.clodagh.com
Photos: Daniel Aubry, New York, NY, USA;
+1 212 414 0014

Orient Retreat Spa
No. 8, Ta Fu Street, Nan Tun District,
Taichung, Taiwan; +866 4 2251 2068;
www.orientretreat.com
Architecture: Robert D. Henry Architects,
New York, NY, USA; +1 212 533 4145;
www.rdh-architects.com
Interiors: Robert D. Henry Architects,
with Thomas Wang Interior Design,
Taipei, Taiwan
Photos: Tim Griffith, San Francisco, CA, USA;
+1 415 640 1419; www.timgriffith.com
Roy Lee, Taipei, Taiwan;
+886 2 2504 8388

The Oriental Spa at The Oriental, Bangkok
48 Oriental Avenue, Bangkok, Thailand;
+66 2 439 7613; www.mandarinoriental.com
Architecture: L'Atelier 10, Bangkok, Thailand;
+66 2 4470 3
Interiors: Morford & Company, Hong Kong;
+852 2525 3131
Photos: George Apostolidis;
www.georgeapostolidis.com
Robert Hubel

Plateau at Grand Hyatt Hong Kong
One Harbor Road, Hong Kong;
+852 2584 7688; www.plateau.com.hk
Design: Morford & Company, Hong Kong;
+852 2525 3131
Photos: Vera Mercer

Quality Spa and Resort Holmsbu
Rødtangveien 18, Holmsbu; +47 32 79 70 00;
www.holmsbuspa.no
Architecture: Halvorsen & Reine, Drammen,
Norway; +47 32 21 52 90; www.heras.no
Interiors: Team Interioret Hanne Hovland,
Oslo, Norway; +47 22 55 07 04
Photos: Christen Raestad, Drammen,
Norway; +47 03 83 92 90

Rajvilas
Goner Road, Jaipur, India;
+91 141 2680101; www.oberoirajvilas.com
Architecture: P.G. Patki & Associates,
Mumbai, India; +91 22 22049182
Interiors: H.L. Lim & Associates,
Singapore; +65 62272872

Red Mountain Resort and Spa
1275 East Red Mountain Circle, Ivins, UT, USA;
+1 435 673 4905; www.redmountainspa.com
Architecture: Rich Wells Architects, St.
George, UT, USA; +1 435 673 4800
Interiors: Gaye Ferraras, Scottsdale, AZ, USA;
+1 480 481 0405; www.ferrarasinteriors.com
Photos: Kim Cornelison

The Retreat at Aphrodite Hills Resort
5 Aphrodite Avenue, Kouklia, Cyprus;
+357 26 828 100; www.aphroditehills.com
Architecture: Wimberly Allison Tong & Goo,
London, UK; +44 20 7906 6600;
www.watg.com
Yiannos Anastasiou Architects, Cyprus;
+357 25 746 322
Interiors: HBA/Hirsch Bedner Associates,
London, UK; +44 20 7925 2099;
www.hbadesign.com
Photos: Polys Pulcherios, Nicosia, Cyprus,
+357 99 699 985

Rogner-Bad Blumau
A-8283 Bad Blumau, Austria;
+43 3383 51000; www.blumau.com
Design: Friedensreich Hundertwasser
Photos: Hans Wiesenhofer

Sámas at Park Hotel Kenmare
Kerry, Ireland; +353 64 41200;
www.parkkenmare.com
Design: Oppermann Associates Architects,
Dublin, Ireland; +353 1 88 99800;
www.oppermann.ie

Sanctuary Spa on Camelback Mountain
5700 East McDonald Drive, Paradise Valley, AZ,
USA; +1 480 948 2100; www.sanctuaryaz.com
Architecture: Allen + Philp Architects,
Scottsdale, AZ, USA; +1 480 990 2800;
www.allenphilp.com
Interiors: Testani Design Troupe,
Scottsdale, AZ, USA; +1 480 945 8200
Photos: Tom Hopkins, Madison, CT, USA;
+1 203 421 4644
Jim Christy, Phoenix, AZ, USA;
+1 602 493 0929; www.jimchristystudio.com

Six Senses Spa at Madinat Jumeirah
Dubai, UAE; +971 4 366 8888;
www.madinatjumeirah.com;
www.sixsenses.com
Architecture: Mirage Mille, Dubai, UAE;
+971 4 366 3993; www.miragemille.com
Interiors: Khuan Chew & Associates, Dubai,
UAE; +971 4 339 1343; www.kca-int.com

Skinklinic
800b Fifth Avenue, New York, NY, USA;
+1 212 521 3100; www.skinklinic.com
Design: Richardson Sadeki, New York,
NY, USA; +1 212 966 0900;
www.richardsonsadeki.com
Photos: Dan Bibb, New York, NY, USA;
+1 212 228 0103

Les Sources de Caudalie
Chemin de Smith Haute Lafitte, Bordeaux-
Martillac, France; +33 5 5783 8383;
www.sources-caudalie.com
Design: Cabinet Collet-Burger, Paris, France;
+33 1 40 92 98 21

Spa at Amelia Island Plantation
6800 First Coast Highway, Amelia Island, FL,
USA; +1 904 432 2220; www.spaamelia.com
Design: Robert D. Henry Architects,
New York, NY, USA; +1 212 533 4145;
www.rdh-architects.com
Photos: Dan Bibb, New York, NY, USA;
+1 212 228 0103
Eric Laignel, Paris, France; +49 1 72 21 44 090

The Spa at Four Seasons Resort Chiang Mai
Mae Rim-Samoeng Old Road, Mae Rim,
Chiang Mai, Thailand; +66 53 298 181;
www.fourseasons.com
Design: Bunnag Architects, Bangkok,
Thailand; +66 2 392 8640
Photos: Luca Tettoni, Singapore;
+65 6323 0402; www.tettoni.com
Robert Miller, Great Falls, VA, USA;
+1 703 472 2316;
www.robertmillerpictures.com

The Spa at Mandarin Oriental, New York
80 Columbus Circle, New York, NY, USA;
+1 212 805 8800; www.mandarinoriental.com
Architecture: Brennan Beer Gorman,
New York, NY, USA; +1 212 888 7663;
www.bbg-bbgm.com
Interiors: HBA/Hirsch Bedner, Atlanta,
GA, USA; +1 404 873 4379;
www.hbadesign.com
Photos: George Apostolidis;
www.georgeapostolidis.com

Spa at Las Ventanas al Paraiso
KM 19.5 Carretera Transpeninsular,
Cabo San Lucas, San Jose Del
Cabo, Baja California Sur,
Mexico; +52 624 144 2800;
www.rosewood-hotels.com
Design: Wilson & Associates, Dallas, TX, USA;
+1 214 521 6753; www.wilsonassoc.com
Landscape: SWA Group, Dallas, TX, USA;
+1 214 954 0016; www.swagroup.com

Spa Bad Elster
Badstrasse 6, Bad Elster, Germany;
+49 374 3771257
Design: Behnisch & Partner, Stuttgart,
Germany; +49 711 607720;
www.behnisch.com
Landscape: Luz and Partner, Stuttgart,
Germany; +49 711 167020
Photos: Christian Kandzia, Stuttgart,
Germany; +49 711 607720;
www.behnisch.com
Martin Schodder, Stuttgart, Germany;
+49 711 7656283

Spa Bellagio
3600 South Las Vegas Boulevard,
Las Vegas, NV, USA; +1 702 693 7472;
www.bellagio.com
Design: Marnell Corrao Associates,
Las Vegas, NV, USA; +1 702 739 2000;
www.marnellcorrao.com
Photos: Robert Mora, Las Vegas, NV,
USA; +1 702 400 1943

Spa Fusion
600 Lantian Road, Pudong, Shanghai, China;
+86 21 5030 8118; www.megafitchina.com
Design: BAU International, Shanghai,
China; +86 21 6431 3335; www.bau.com.au
Photos: Freeline Advertising

Spa Without Walls at The Fairmont Orchid
One North Kaniku Drive, Kohala Coast,
HI, USA; +1 808 885 2000;
www.fairmont.com
Design: Wimberly Allison Tong & Goo,
Honolulu, HI, USA; +1 808 521 8888;
www.watg.com
Photos: Wally Krysciak, Richmond Hill,
ON, Canada; +1 905 764 5594

Takaragawa Onsen
1899 Fujiwara Minikami-lown, Tone-Gun
Gunma-Pref., Japan; +81 278 75 2611;
www.takaragawa.com

Thalassa Spa
Anassa, Latsi, Polis, Cyprus;
+357 2 888 000; www.thanoshotels.com
Architecture: Sandy & Babcock International,
San Francisco, CA, USA; +1 415 673 8990;
www.sandybabcock.com
Interiors: James Northcutt Associates
(now Wilson & Associates), Los Angeles,
CA, USA; +1 323 651 3234;
www.wilsonassoc.com
Photos: Henri Del Olmo, Nice, France;
+33 4 9392 1603

Thermae Bath Spa
The Hetting Pump Room, Hot Bath Street,
Bath, UK; +44 1225 33 1234;
www.thermaebathspa.com
Architecture: Nicholas Grimshaw & Partners,
London, UK; +44 20 7291 4141;
www.grimshaw-architects.com
Restoration: Donald Insall Associates, London,
UK; +44 20 7245 9888;
www.insall-bath.co.uk
Photos: Edmund Sumner, London, UK;
+44 20 7601 6477;
www.edmundsumner.co.uk
Nick Smith; +07 973 392001;
www.nicksmithphotography.com
Matt Cardy

Therme Vals
7132 Vals/GR, Switzerland;
+41 81 926 80 80; www.therme-vals.ch
Design: Peter Zumthor, Haldenstein,
Switzerland; +41 081 354 9292
Photos: Tim Griffith, San Francisco, CA, USA;
+1 415 640 1419; www.timgriffith.com
Henry Pierre Schultz, Zurich, Switzerland;
+41 1 251 26 25; www.henrypierreschultz.ch

Vigilius Mountain Resort
Vigiljoch 39011, Lana, Italy;
+39 0473 556 600; www.vigilius.com
Architecture: Matteo Thun, Milan, Italy;
+39 02 655 691; www.matteothun.com
Photos: Christine Schaum, Munich, Germany,
+49 89 2303 2977
Augustin Ochsenreiter, Bozen, Italy;
+39 6 71 97 61 47
Thierry Malty, Paris, France;
+33 1 43 58 63 63

Zara Spa
Dead Sea Road, Amman, Jordan;
+962 5 3561111;
www.movenpick-deadsea.com
Architecture: Wimberly Allison Tong & Goo,
London, UK; +44 20 7906 6600;
www.watg.com
Ammar Khammash, Amman, Jordan;
+962 6 5695134; www.khammash.com
Interiors: Ammar Khammash, Amman,
Jordan; +962 6 5695134;
www.khammash.com
Photos: Jan Kassay, Amman, Jordan;
+962 6 4622581

Acknowledgements

Our thanks and gratitude go to those who lent their expertise and talents to the chapter introductions for this book: Julie Iovine for her delight in spa history; Jonathan Paul de Vierville for his passion for thermalism; Bernie Burt for his exhaustive knowledge; Roger Gabriel for his commitment to healing; Shenyn Wang for her insight and savvy; Sonu Shivdasani for grasping the world of the senses; Dan Fryda for delving into the depths of the sea; and Michael Adams for his genuine hospitality.
—Robert D. Henry and Julie D. Taylor

The individuals who make up the Spa Industry are caregivers, kudos for your healing touch and the constant reminder to connect with our sensuous side. A special thanks to Julie Taylor who revived a five-year effort and who made this project happen with her creativity, passion, and rigor along with Rebecca Wu Norman whose diligence and humor were most vital ingredients. Thank you Paul Latham, Alessina Brooks, and The Images Publishing Group for your spirited pep talks, skillful guidance, and your faith in our project. Indebtedness goes to Ethyl Chaney, my nurturing high-school English teacher for imparting professional direction, and most importantly my family, Nancy Wu, Bo and Chloe, who bring compassion and life to my years.
—Robert D. Henry

Thanks to Bob Henry for his creative spark for this book, and to Paul Latham and Alessina Brooks at The Images Publishing Group for giving us the opportunity to make it a reality. Also at Images, Robyn Beaver and Joe Boschetti have been allies and colleagues for so long, that it's great to work with them on an original creation. Rebecca Wu Norman at Robert D. Henry Architects was tremendously organized and patient with the mounds of materials (and with my many requests). Only with my great team at Taylor & Company could I have dared to take on this project. Melissa Tchirkow, Anne Dickhoff, and Nina Tronstein continue to amaze and delight me, and keep me and our office going strong.
—Julie D. Taylor

Robert D. Henry

Award-winning architect Robert D. Henry
has been studying the art of spas for
15 years, and boasts of having more than
300 spa treatments from around the globe.
He applies the "architecture of the senses"
to the spas, resorts, lounges, and residences
he designs through his firm Robert D. Henry
Architects in New York City. Among his
more recognized projects are the Spa at
Wynn Resort in Las Vegas, the Spa at the
Mar-A-Lago Club in Palm Beach, and
Potion Lounge in New York City. Henry's
work is widely published, and he is a popular
international speaker to the spa and
hospitality industries.

Julie D. Taylor

Design and spa aficionado Julie D. Taylor is the
principal of Taylor & Company, a Los Angeles-
based public relations and communications
firm specializing in architecture, design,
building, and creative industries. She was
formerly a magazine editor, and is the author
of *Outdoor Rooms* and *Bars, Pubs, Cafés*,
as well as numerous articles about design,
art, and architecture. Taylor lectures on
the promotion of design for organizations
and universities.

Photo: Jimmy Cohrssen

Photo: Sue Tallon